What People Are Saying

"The Upside to Bipolar: 7 Steps to Heal Your Disorder is a powerful testament to one woman's extraordinary resilience and what can happen when we believe healing is possible."
Wendy Beth Cozzens, Soul guided coaching, #1 international best-selling author

"This book will give you a new perspective of what is important for your brain health: from foundational micronutrients to mindfulness and yoga, and from exercise to adopting a healing mindset. Buy this book and reclaim your mental health!"
Bonnie J. Kaplan, PhD, coauthor of The Better Brain

"Michelle Reittinger takes us to the threshold of possibility, where bipolarity is redefined—not as a life sentence or stigma, but as a space brimming with hope and learning."
Sophie Rouméas, transgenerational & mindfulness coach, hypnosis practitioner

"Michelle is such an inspiration! This book and Michelle's journey can be helpful to people who struggle with a variety of mental health issues, not just bipolar disorder! The book really shows that with effort, persistence, and support, it really is possible to live well after a mental health diagnosis. The hope this offers is invaluable."
Julie Sickles, LCSW

"For individuals living with bipolar disorder, Michelle's book is a beacon of hope and a practical guide. Mental health professionals will also find The Upside of Bipolar to be an enriching resource."
Dr Jennifer Giordano, psychiatrist

"Her honesty, determination, and even skepticism when approaching new ideas made me trust her more as a legitimate source of helpful information."
Mequell Buck – Author, suicide survivor and founder of Mental Illness Warrior

"...the gift of her story: it replaces a narrative of illness told by psychiatry today with a narrative of recovery and healing."
Robert Whitaker, Author of *Anatomy of an Epidemic* and *Mad in America*

"The birth of resilience! Michelle authenticates to the reader how important it was for her to relentlessly search for a holistic alternative solution and found it. She put together a very comprehensive, well laid out plan to help and support anyone suffering. Everyone needs to experience her struggle and triumph!"
Jason M. Palmer, Master horse trainer, #1 international best-selling author

"This book is a game changer for its holistic and healing approach. This is a must buy, read and share with anyone you care about living with bipolar disorder."
Maureen Ryan Blake, Maureen Ryan Blake Media and #1 international best-selling author

THE UPSIDE OF BIPOLAR

7 Steps to Heal Your Disorder

A Research-Based, Integrated Method for Healing and Recovery

Michelle Reittinger

The Upside of Bipolar:
7 Steps to Heal Your Disorder
A Research-Based, Integrated Method for Healing and Recovery

Inspired Legacy Publishing is a division of (DBA) Inspired Legacy, LLC
PO Box 900816
Sandy UT 84090-0816.

Changing Names & Medical Advice
Some names and identifying details have been changed to protect the privacy of individuals.
This book is not intended as a substitute for the medical advice of physicians. The reader
should regularly consult a physician in matters relating to his/her health and particularly
with respect to any symptoms that may require diagnosis or medical attention.

ISBN 979-8-9915644-0-3 (paperback)
ISBN 979-8-9915644-1-0 (hardcover)

Printed in the United States of America.

Contents

A letter to the reader

Dear Reader,

How did you feel when you received your bipolar diagnosis? Was it as devastating as receiving a life sentence? I know it was for me. I felt broken and damaged—who would ever want me like this?

It wasn't just what the doctor said. Everything that I read about bipolar online reinforced the hopelessness. Countless social media accounts focused on bringing "awareness" to what it was like to experience mania or depression in an attempt to *normalize* the symptoms.

I witnessed celebrities diagnosed with bipolar who had very public meltdowns, exhibiting bizarre, humiliating behavior. Movies and television shows portrayed characters with bipolar as persistently ill victims, destroying everything in their path—relationships, careers, and even their own lives.

Like me early on, you may have concluded that the best you can expect out of life with bipolar is learning to "suffer well" with it.

But I am here to tell you that is not true!

My experience following the industry's traditional treatment plan—obediently taking psychotropic drugs—for the first twelve years after my diagnosis was disastrous. Nothing worked; in fact, as I became progressively worse, my doctors dismissed this as the natural course of the "disorder." I was told bipolar was:

- a chemical imbalance,
- like having diabetes and medication is like insulin, and
- chronic and incurable.

At the time I had no reason to doubt them. That all changed when I discovered an integrated treatment model that uncovered the *root causes of my bipolar symptoms and addressed them at their source*. I am not exaggerating when I say I found a realistic, powerful path to healing my brain!

For years I lived with intense shame, embarrassment, and guilt over the irrational decisions I made when I was in a manic or depressed state. But today, the healing I have experienced is so complete that I can view the past with compassion and forgiveness. I'm also capable of being fully present in the inherent gifts in this day so I can face any challenge with balance and joy. Now, I can truly look to the future with genuine hope and optimism. I believe this is possible for you as well!

Why am I writing this to you? When I first discovered it was possible to heal bipolar, I felt angry, betrayed, robbed, and lied to by the very industry that I had turned to for help when I first became sick. All of the tools that I had discovered had been thoroughly researched and proven to be effective at treating the underlying causes of bipolar symptoms. So why had I been left to figure this all out by myself?

As I recognized the suffering of tens of thousands of others who still believed the lies we have been told about bipolar, my anger faded and evolved into steadfast determination. I was compelled to share what I have discovered with you so that you, too, can learn how to heal.

In this book I will:

- Take you a bit on my own journey so you know that you are not alone in what you're facing now, and what you may have been facing since your diagnosis. Too many of us have lacked a partner in this struggle, and that ends now.
- Guide you through the research that not only refutes but disproves the myths and false beliefs in the industry about bipolar. These trusted sources show you the truth about what is causing your bipolar symptoms so you are educated, not helpless.
- Help you learn how to *listen* to what your symptoms are trying to tell you and respond using research-based tools that will resolve your symptoms at their source.
- Teach you how to become so self-aware that you can take back control of your mind, your body, and your life as you move forward on the path to healing.
- Show you how to trust your intuition and access the power within your

own mind and body to heal without having to use medications to cover up your symptoms—or worse yet, introduce new ones. You will learn how to become your own best advocate, and utilize the gifts already inside of you . . . to thrive.

This book is *not* about learning how to *manage or live with your bipolar symptoms*—this book teaches you how to *heal and recover from your bipolar symptoms*. It is the treatment plan I wish *I* had been given over two decades ago.

Bipolar doesn't have to be a life sentence! I almost didn't make it, but I am now proud to say I went from feeling despair and hopelessness to living a joyful, purposeful life. This is why I've written this book, with great compassion and understanding, to show you how we can do the same together.

Now I invite you on the journey of self-discovery to find the naturally remarkable and empowered human being you were meant to be. It starts here.

Part 1
My Story

CHAPTER 1

WAKING UP TO A NIGHTMARE

"Hey, check out Barfman's shoes!" came the unmistakable voice of Gabe Jackson in my first period classroom. "What'd you do, go dumpster diving for them?"

I looked down in horror as I realized I had forgotten to change my shoes that morning when I finished my paper route because I was running late, *again*. I felt sick when I saw my dirty, holey, knockoff Keds on display for everyone to see.

As the entire class laughed, I looked pleadingly at my teacher for help. He just looked annoyed and told me to take my seat. As I walked slowly to my desk in the back row, I wished desperately that I could somehow hide my feet . . . maybe even the rest of me too.

I also noticed I'd missed some ink on my fingers when I'd hurriedly washed my hands after rolling the newspapers that morning in the dark. As I rubbed my fingers to get rid of the ink, I thought in frustration, *I only started this stupid paper route so I could buy some new clothes for myself!*

In my second period class, Jessica looked pointedly at my shoes and then snidely asked, "Why do you wear such lame clothes, anyway?"

I tugged subconsciously at my hand-me-down polo shirt. Almost everything I owned was secondhand. Every pair of pants were highwaters on my tall, skinny body, and none of it was name brand.

"Well," I started uncomfortably, "I'm the oldest of eight kids and my mom doesn't work so we can't afford expensive clothes."

She laughed derisively at me and said, "That's stupid! The Nielsens have eight kids and they all wear Esprit and Levi!"

Her words stung because I knew it was true.

Things went from bad to worse, though, when I discovered in my third period class that I was failing math. My heart sank as I realized this would make me ineligible to try out for the drill team. I wanted so *desperately* to be on the drill team because then maybe someone would want to be my friend. As I sat there, I realized that I had been lonely for four years! Was it really all because of my clothes, or was there something just wrong with me?

Each year we had moved, forcing me to start at a new school, trying to make new friends . . . trying to find my place and where I fit in. Only I felt like that square peg trying desperately to fit into round holes, and the kids never let me forget it.

The worst had been last fall at this new school, when one of the most popular boys had walked beside me on the way to the park, whispering in my ear that he liked me. Me? A boy actually liked me! I didn't know it was an elaborate setup until the next day when my new "friends" humiliated me in the lunchroom.

"Dummy!" one of the girls had said loudly. "He likes Lisa; he just asked her to be his girlfriend. Why would Sam like a skinny dork like you?"

So today, like every day since then, I headed to the library where I ate alone.

My nightmare day ended with me being held after my final class by my English teacher. When my teacher finally dismissed me, I ran to the front of the school to discover the parking lot nearly empty. I couldn't believe it; I had missed my ride home.

As I began the forty-five minute walk home through my Northern California town, my heart ached. I looked down with blurry eyes at the hated sneakers on my feet as they scattered the gravel on the side of the road. *Why doesn't anyone like me?* my broken heart asked.

The spring breeze blew the smell of fresh cut grass, something that usually delighted me, but all I could think was, *I hate myself! What is wrong with me?*

At times, I had too much energy and people would say, in annoyance, "Stop being so loud!" At other times, I felt an intense sadness that felt like a heavy weight in my chest. Why couldn't I find a happy medium, a balanced place where I was just happy and accepted?

I had always believed in my soul that there was a God, but when I was awash in this overwhelming darkness, I couldn't feel Him. My only conclusion was, *I must have done something bad to feel this way.* Desperately, I looked for evidence in my life of what I had done wrong to separate me from my Heavenly Father. Then I would find a way to punish myself, usually making myself do extra, secret chores.

As I trudged along the road, my mind filled with relentless, penetrating voices:

You are ugly! You are loud! You are stupid! You are undisciplined! You're always late! You always lose everything! No one likes you! You are worthless!

And on and on and on . . . until suddenly came the loudest voice of all:

I want to die!

When that thought came into my mind, it pervaded my entire being. I really didn't want to live anymore. I wanted the pain to end. I began sobbing now, not caring if the people driving by noticed. I was now only twenty minutes from home—but it didn't matter. No one cared about me anyway. My chest became tight and I couldn't breathe. I wrapped my arms tightly around myself and doubled over, choking on a sob.

That's why it was so shocking when suddenly into my darkness came a sweet, pleading voice that pierced through the shadows and touched my mind and my heart.

"Mommy, please don't say that!"

Somewhere deep inside me, I knew that voice. It was my daughter's voice. My unborn daughter. That was physically impossible as I was years away from becoming a parent, and I didn't know *how* I knew it, but I was sure it was true. Love flooded over my entire body. Astonished, I could breathe again, and an emotion that I hadn't experienced in a long time rose up in my chest. Hope. It was hope. I wanted to live . . . for *her.*

It was the first time my daughter would save my life.

When I finally arrived home that day, even though my energy had lifted, my mother couldn't help but notice my tear-stained face and asked me what happened. I opened my broken heart to my mother about the cruelty of kids and she listened with great compassion.

When I was finished, she looked at me thoughtfully and said, "You know, I bet there are other kids at school who are lonely like you. Why don't you find them and be their friend?"

As she hugged me tightly, I thought with hope, *I can't wait to be a mother like my mom!*

My mom's kind suggestion led me to find Christine, Kristen, and Allison. We were all social outcasts—a little band of misfit toys. We found refuge in each other and those friendships helped me survive my last year of junior high.

With these new companions, I began to develop a new "skill"; I became a chameleon. I liked whatever they liked, listened to the music they listened to, and watched the same movies. I was resolved to keep these friends no matter what!

When I began high school, I found another respite from the storm: swim team. Club swim team was too expensive so I had to wait until high school to begin. I was terrible at first; my coach literally laughed at me when I tried out because although I had always been a fish in the water, I had never been taught the competitive strokes. What I lacked in skill I made up for with grit and determination. My freshman year I was awarded "most improved swimmer," and by my senior year, I was named team captain and "most valuable swimmer."

After graduating in 1992, I was recruited to swim for a local junior college and that was where I really began to blossom! As a freshman, I was named a team captain. I broke one individual record, was on three relays that broke school records, and I was named All-American–ranked in the top one hundred in the nation–in seven events.

My teammates, who became my best friends, were excellent students and encouraged me in my studies. My second semester in college I earned straight As! I had never been happier in my life. I finally felt like I was good enough. That was when I met my prince.

Alex was a six-foot, four-inch, blond-haired, blue-eyed Adonis. He checked every box and then some. When we were first dating, he treated me like a queen. He opened my doors, spoke respectfully to me, and told me all the time how beautiful I was—just like my dad treated my mom. He was religiously devout and came from what appeared to be an ideal family.

When he asked me to marry him three months later, I felt my dreams were finally coming true! We were married after a brief three-month engagement on October 15, 1993.

Getting married at nineteen wasn't a red flag for anyone in my family because my mother was married at the same age. In fact, I was proud. In marrying Alex, I believed I had hit the jackpot, and I couldn't wait to become a mother! I couldn't wait to finally meet the little girl whose voice had saved my life several years prior.

Two weeks after we were married, I was in the kitchen doing dishes one afternoon. I was smiling and humming a favorite song when Alex walked in. He stood there looking at me for a moment, and my heart warmed under his gaze. Then he casually asked, "Have you ever thought about divorce?"

I stood frozen in stunned silence, gripping the dish in my hands.

After a few more moments, he followed up with, "I just always thought if I got married and it didn't work out, I would get divorced." I felt like he had smacked me and tears welled up in my eyes, spilling over into the sink. Why was he saying this to me?

When he noticed the tears, he apologized to me. "Hey, hey don't cry," he said, sounding slightly annoyed. "I was only thinking out loud." He patted me on the back a couple times and then walked away.

A week later, we were sitting at our little dining room table eating dinner when out of the blue my husband commented, "You know, you're really not my type."

I stared at him, startled by his declaration and feeling like he'd struck me again.

He then proceeded to describe his ideal woman–long dark hair, voluptuous soft chest, and gorgeous, curvy hips–opposite of me in every way. And then I heard him say, "Oh man, don't cry again. I'm just thinking out loud! You're so sensitive!"

What was I supposed to think? Sometime later, I would overhear my dad describe my experience to a friend, "It was like she went to bed to a dream and woke up to a nightmare."

Soon he was isolating me from family and friends. One day while he was at work, I had rollerbladed over to visit two friends from high school who had rented an apartment near ours. When I got home, Alex was sitting in the living room waiting for me. "Where were you?" he demanded.

"Um," I stammered in confusion. "I went to see Audra and Leslie's new apartment."

"Married people don't go hang out with their single friends," he lectured.

"But what about your friend Nate who came over last week for dinner?" I challenged timidly.

"That's different because we were together. Don't do it again!" Alex stalked out of the room, ending the conversation. I stopped visiting my friends after that.

Even worse, we only lived twenty minutes away from my parents and my nine younger siblings, but I never saw them. Alex wouldn't allow me to visit them alone, and on the rare occasion that we did visit, I was so nervous about saying or doing something he didn't like that I couldn't relax around my own family.

One evening my dad showed up at my apartment with flowers. "Hey, Shelly Belle," he said cheerfully. "I was thinking about you and wanted to bring you flowers on my way home from work!"

Astonished, I quickly accepted the bouquet and hugged him tightly. I knew it wasn't *really* on his way and my heart swelled with love for my kind, gentle father. I longed so much to leave with him, to be with my daddy and feel loved and cherished, just for a little while.

When he left, I closed the door and Alex stalked over. "Why is your dad bringing you flowers?" he questioned accusingly. "What have you been saying to him?"

"I don't know why he came," I replied shakily. "It's just something he likes to do. I haven't talked to him in weeks, I promise!"

Alex stared at me coldly for what felt like forever and then finally left the room.

Completely isolated from family and friends now, the nightmare really began. Alex started watching pornographic movies. At first I would leave when he turned them on, but soon he wouldn't let me go because he wanted to do what he watched on the screen to me. I quickly learned that saying no was not an option. Crying made things worse.

Ten months into my marriage, we were driving home from spending the evening with one of my best friends from high school and her husband. We'd had fun playing games and I was elated and relieved that my husband finally liked one of my friends enough to hang out.

He told me that it was "appropriate" because they were another married couple. Street lights cast shadows on the ground as we drove along. I looked out the car window and felt a surge of hope that maybe things were finally going to get better between us.

Suddenly, my husband pulled the car into a vacant parking lot. Without a word, he turned the car off. I was so surprised I didn't know what to say, but as I watched his hands grip and release the steering wheel, my chest got tight and my stomach started to constrict. *Oh no. Something is wrong,* I thought. Confused, my mind raced back over every detail of the night in hopes of a clue about what I'd done to upset him.

I couldn't think of anything. Alex seemed really happy all night. Happier than I'd seen him in months, in fact. He was so charming and friendly with Lisa and James, just like he'd been when we were dating and first married. What was going on? What had flipped the switch?

Finally, he spoke. "Do you know why I like hanging out with the Jensens? It's because I'm attracted to Lisa."

I felt sick. I knew why the moment he admitted it. Lisa was very well-endowed. She had developed early, and it had made her very popular with the boys in high school. I looked down at my flat chest and tears of shame and embarrassment rolled down my hot cheeks. I didn't know how to respond.

"I don't love you," he said coldly, "and I don't want to be married anymore."

And that was it. Without another word, he turned on the ignition and pulled back out onto the street. As I wept, I struggled not to let him hear since he hated it when I cried. Blinded by my tears, I didn't realize that we weren't driving back to our apartment anymore. Instead, Alex headed for my parents' house.

It was past 1:30 in the morning when he dropped me off and drove away without a glance back. I stood frozen for a minute in shame and humiliation, not sure what to do. The house was dark and silent; my parents and younger siblings were asleep. The neighborhood was quiet, but it was too cold to stand there much longer. Finally, I walked up to the door and knocked. If I didn't ring the doorbell, maybe I wouldn't wake my younger brothers and sisters.

As I waited in the dark, I suddenly lost control. Sobs racked my body and I pounded harder, desperate for *someone* to help me. I was sure my heart was literally shattering into millions of pieces. Light cut through the darkness, beckoning me to safety as my dad opened the door.

"Michelle?" he questioned, confusion and concern coloring his tone.

I fell into my father's arms crying convulsively, trying to speak but unable to calm myself enough to get the words out.

I don't remember much about the rest of that night. All I know is I cried myself to sleep, lying on my mother's lap on the couch. The next day, I had no more tears. I had gone completely numb inside.

After only a week apart, Alex apologized and charmed me into giving him another chance. The honeymoon period was blissful. He talked lovingly about starting our family and my heart yearned for my daughter.

Over the next three months, however, I recognized it was all an act. The stark truth when his true colors would seep through was that I didn't want children with this man. I knew without a shadow of a doubt that any children I brought into our home would suffer the same treatment or perhaps worse. The petrifying thought of my little girl having Alex for a father gave me the courage I needed. I left one week before Christmas, 1994, and even though I was still numb inside, for the first time in a long time, I could breathe.

CHAPTER 2

LIKE WATCHING A RUNAWAY TRAIN

When my family became aware of my decision to separate from Alex, they rallied around me like powerful warriors. Their support and love enveloped me, giving me much-needed strength.

After all, they had witnessed my pain and my husband's behavior over the past year and a half. Mom and Dad encouraged me to seek counseling or join a support group. I resisted defiantly. I didn't ever want to talk to *anyone* about the hell I had survived. I didn't want it to define me—I just wanted to move on with my life. But the shadows continued to haunt me.

In January of 1995, I moved from California to Utah and enrolled at Brigham Young University. My parents had met and married while attending this school and I dreamed my entire life of following in their footsteps. I hoped that this would be a new beginning for me, but deep inside, I felt damaged.

I wanted so much to be asked on a date, but dreaded having to tell any man that I was divorced. There was a stigma surrounding divorce in my religious culture, especially at such a young age. Marriage was supposed to last forever. The darkness I'd felt as a teenager returned with a vengeance. One night I was supposed to be studying for a test, but instead I found myself wandering the cold campus, alone in the dark, crying for hours. Something had to change.

I was determined to fix myself. One day when I was in the campus bookstore, I noticed a "self-help" section and bought a book that caught my eye, *Seven Habits of Highly Effective People*. Despite my drive to get better, I never made it past the first chapter, and my mental state continued to deteriorate.

After a year at BYU, I transferred to the University of Utah in Salt Lake City. *All I need is a fresh start*, I told myself, *and then I'll be okay*. But the gloominess continued to be something I couldn't shake.

Over the next two years, I experienced increasingly erratic mood swings. I would have weeks when I was animated, full of enthusiasm and determination, coming up with a new life plan and telling everyone I met about it. One semester I switched my major *six times*. That wasn't the only radical shift. I would make drastic changes to my hair. My stylist loved me because I would go into appointments and say, "Do whatever you want!" Once I ended up with a one-inch pixie cut, dyed platinum blonde.

I'd feel high on life one moment, then I would feel myself descending into darkness. Being around other people was exhausting–trying to pretend I was "normal" when I felt like I was swimming through tar. I would struggle to get out of bed, skip my classes, and watch hours of television. During those periods, I felt ugly inside and out and would buy new makeup, trying to make myself feel better.

My parents, who had moved to Washington state near Seattle, grew concerned as the mood swings became more pronounced and noticeable. During my ups, I would call them multiple times a week, speaking rapidly and animatedly about my new life plans. Then suddenly the calls would stop, and they wouldn't hear from me for weeks. By the next call, I had an entirely different life plan.

They finally urged me to see a psychiatrist. At first I resisted, I was afraid of being told I was "broken," but the more intense the mood swings became, the more I became convinced that I needed help. I ultimately relented.

One spring weekday, I found myself sitting in the waiting room of the psychiatrist's office filling out a pile of forms. I didn't really want to be there, but my parents had pleaded with me to go. My aunt, who lived nearby, was kind enough to bring me and was sitting quietly next to me while I struggled with the forms.

Family History

What do I put here? I wondered, letting the pen hover over the paper for a moment. *My grandmother was in the hospital a lot growing up, but no one ever talked about what she was sick with. She also mentioned her therapist frequently, saying "my therapist said this" or "my therapist said that"---to the point I was convinced I was NEVER going to go to a therapist!* I shuddered and left that spot blank.

History of Alcoholism

My great uncle was an alcoholic; do I write that?

I felt overwhelmed by so many pages of questions and marking far too many boxes.

I feel bad like I am a failure and I've let everyone down:

- ¤ **Never**
- ¤ **Once in a while**
- ¤ **More than half the time**
- ¤ **All the time**

I hate these questions! Of course I am a failure; just look at my life!

I was terrified of being diagnosed with a mental illness! Over the past three years, I had purchased several self-help books, but each time I never made it past the first chapter. My experience with swimming had convinced me that I could overcome my problems with goal setting and hard work, but nothing was working!

After turning in the questionnaire, my aunt and I were escorted into the psychiatrist's office. There was a desk in the corner cluttered with papers and books, and I stood there for a moment, looking around, unsure of where to position myself.

A man who looked to be at least twice my age stood just inside the doorway and smiled warmly at me. "You can sit in whatever seat makes you feel most comfortable," he offered kindly.

That was a joke; no seat in the world could make me feel comfortable right now. I chose a seat in a corner by a Ficus with a chair next to it for my aunt.

"What brings you here today?" he asked.

I didn't really know where to start. What did he want to know? I couldn't think of what to say and instead, tears silently rolled down my face. It was all too much. I hunched over, wanting to curl into a ball. My brain felt like mud. I could hear my aunt saying something to the doctor, but it sounded far away.

I don't want to live like this anymore! I thought in desperation. Graduation was only a month away and I hadn't been attending my classes. I had so much work to do and I didn't know how I could ever get it all done on time.

Maybe I'll get lucky and get a burst of energy that keeps me up for days! I thought hopefully. Last time that happened I had done an entire semester's work in a couple of days and ended up on the dean's list.

That's such a bad habit, came the self-reproach in my mind. *Why can't I just study consistently like everyone else?*

I could hear the doctor asking a question and stared at him dully. *What did he just say?* None of it was registering.

What if he says there's nothing wrong with me? I worried. *That would be so humiliating. Then it really would all be my fault.*

I could barely breathe. *What if he tells me there* is *something wrong with me? I'm defective, damaged. No one will want me like that!* I thought, panic rising in my chest.

Wait, what did he just say? I looked up and said timidly, embarrassed by my distraction, "I'm sorry, could you repeat that?"

The doctor looked at me sympathetically from behind his wire-rimmed glasses, rocking forward in his brown swivel chair and said gently, "You have depression and anxiety disorders. They are chemical imbalances in the brain, and with the right medication, you will feel much better."

My aunt put her hand on my back and patted me reassuringly as the doctor wrote out a prescription for an antidepressant and handed it to me. After giving me instructions for how to begin taking the medication, he asked me to make a follow-up appointment with the receptionist on the way out.

As my aunt and I exited the building into the afternoon sunlight, I suddenly felt like a huge weight had been lifted from my shoulders.

This isn't my fault after all! I thought with relief. As I listened to the birds singing in the trees, I believed, for the first time in years, that there was hope for me.

This is it! The answer I've been searching for all this time. All I needed was the right medication and I would be okay.

One month later, I stood in a sea of black caps and gowns. *I can't believe I did it!* I thought in amazement and relief as I waited in line to walk into my commencement ceremony on University of Utah campus.

There was a tangible enthusiasm in the warm June air as the graduates all around me spoke animatedly to each other while we waited to enter the arena. Three weeks ago, I had experienced the hoped-for burst of energy and spent three days in a row without sleep, completing all of my coursework. Now, I was graduating from college!

As the line inched forward, I contemplated my future. My parents had convinced me to move back home after graduation to give me a chance to get stable. The medication I was taking didn't seem to be making much difference yet. In my follow-up appointment with my doctor, he had explained that it would take a few months for the antidepressant to build up in my system and to be patient.

I was looking forward to being at home again. Six of my younger brothers and sisters were still living with my parents and I missed them terribly. I also didn't know yet what I wanted to do for a career, and this would give me time to figure out my next step.

My hands touched the heart-shaped jade pendant my parents had given me as a graduation gift. "We're so proud of you!" my dad had said with sincere admiration in his voice. "You have been through so much and yet you persevered. This is such a tremendous accomplishment, Michelle."

My heart swelled with gratitude for my parents' support and encouragement. Even if I didn't know my exact direction yet, I was looking forward to the future with hope. The rest of the day was a blur of speeches, pictures, and celebrations. Then it was time to pack up and head home to Washington.

I found a new doctor soon after moving to Seattle, and, based on the information I provided, she concurred with my initial diagnosis–anxiety and depression. Over the following six months, however, my mood swings became more pronounced–this time my parents had a front row seat to the show.

Between June and December, I went through three jobs, fell in love and had my heart broken twice, then came up with two new life plans that involved moving to other states where I knew no one. My father stopped me one day, his voice filled with sincere concern, "Michelle, it's like watching a runaway train!"

He and my mom implored me to speak with my psychiatrist and gave me a list of concerning symptoms they were observing: rapid, animated speech, sudden shifts in plans that were irrational and impulsive, and emotionally driven behavior. Armed with this new insight and determined to conquer this latest complication, I made an appointment to see my doctor.

"You've been misdiagnosed," I heard my psychiatrist say from behind her large wooden desk, piled with stacks of patient files and papers. I had been staring at the wall behind her that held all of her degrees and certifications.

"Misdiagnosed?" I asked in confusion, refocusing my attention on her. "How did that happen?"

She looked over her black, plastic reading glasses and explained, "You have bipolar two disorder with rapid cycling, which is often misdiagnosed as anxiety and depression because the symptoms are so similar. The mistake was revealed as the antidepressants built up in your system and exacerbated your hypomania."

Bipolar? I thought with alarm. *Aren't people with bipolar crazy and dangerous?*

"What is 'bipolar two' disorder?" I asked with some apprehension.

"It is similar to bipolar one because you experience mood shifts between depression and an elevated mood state called hypomania; however, unlike bipolar one, you never reach a full manic state or experience psychosis."

I shifted uncomfortably in my chair. I didn't know much about bipolar, but I remembered reading and watching "One Flew Over the Cuckoo's Nest" in high school, which horrified me, and hearing about people with bipolar in the news.

My doctor, unaware of my worries, reassured me, "Now that we understand what we're dealing with, we can get you on the right medications and you're going to feel much better."

I glanced back up at her wall of degrees and I prayed that she was right.

With the new diagnosis came new medication, and within a week, my first experience with the side effects of psychotropic drugs. It was a gray, drizzly winter day in Washington, and I felt chilled to my bone as I stepped on the bus to go to work in Seattle.

I had been blessed with a wonderful new job as an executive assistant to the chief legal counsel for Plum Creek Timber Company based in downtown Seattle. I was so thrilled with this new position. At age twenty-four, I felt so grown up and professional, desperate to prove myself to my new boss. That morning I'd woken up with a terrible headache, but I didn't want to miss work and make a bad impression by calling in sick after only a few weeks at my job.

As I stared out the window at the traffic on the forty-minute bus ride, however, my head began to throb. When we neared my destination, without warning, I began to experience an alarming sensation. I thought I could feel every neuron and synapse in my brain disconnecting, like some invisible hand was going through my head unplugging the connections. There was a snap and a fizzing sensation with each disconnection, like the opening of a can of soda.

Pop! Fizzz . . . Pop! Fizzz . . . Pop! Fizzz . . . Over and over, it kept repeating throughout my brain.

Am I going crazy? I thought frantically. I looked around at the other people on the bus. Could they see what was happening to me?

My bus stop was still two blocks away, but desperately I yanked the cord. The driver pulled over and I quickly disembarked without making eye contact with anyone. As I walked at a rapid pace down the street, I started to cry. Every cell in my body began vibrating as my brain continued to disconnect from itself. I couldn't let anyone at my new job know about the chaos happening inside my skull. They would fire me! But I had to do something.

As I entered the elevator, I avoided eye contact with anyone, afraid they'd see something was wrong with me. I got off on my floor and hurried to my cubicle. I was so thankful it was tucked away in a corner where I could hide. I prayed silently that no one would hear me. In a hushed voice, I called my mom.

"Hello?"

Hearing her voice I choked on a sob. "Mom, help me. I think I'm going crazy!"

"Michelle?" she replied, her voice full of concern. "What's the matter?"

"I can feel all the synapses in my brain," I said in a hoarse, panicked whisper. "And they are disconnecting! I'm going crazy! Please help me!"

"Let me call Dad and I'll call you right back," Mom insisted. "Just hang on, okay?"

I tried to swallow before whispering, "Okay."

I hung up the phone and literally got down on my hands and knees to crawl under my desk. I couldn't stop crying. It felt like forever before the phone finally rang.

"Hello?" I managed, my voice barely audible.

"Michelle, it's Mom. Your dad just got out of his meeting and he is leaving work now to come pick you up and bring you home." Her voice was calm and reassuring. "He'll be there in fifteen minutes."

"Mom, I'm so scared! I think my brain is *breaking*!" I could feel myself becoming hysterical.

"I know, sweetheart," she replied, her tone firm but comforting. "Try to breathe. It's going to be okay. Dad is on his way."

I got back under the desk, arms wrapped tightly around my chest, trying to hold myself together, and waited for Dad to arrive. By now I felt like I was going to jump out of my skin. Thankfully, no one on the floor came near my cubicle.

This was the first of a stream of adverse reactions to medications. I began to hate taking any medication because it never really helped, and the side effects were terrible. Even so, the doctors convinced me that bipolar disorder was like having diabetes, and psychotropic medication was akin to insulin. If that was true, though, why did they keep changing my medications? And why wasn't anything working?

In spite of these deep and life-altering questions, I kept going to my appointments, taking every drug that was prescribed because I was told that was my only hope of getting better. Unfortunately, my symptoms still persisted and I created a pattern of burning bridges and starting over. The idea that had first formed in junior high crept back into my mind: *there is something wrong with me. I'm broken.*

My unbalanced mind kept seeking relief in change. I was able to maintain that job for a year and a half while I moved three times and fell in and out of love two more times. Five months after I began working for Plum Creek, I moved into a house with roommates, but it only lasted for six months before I was back in with my parents. After another six months with them, I moved back out into an apartment with yet another new roommate.

Soon after my third move, I became bored with my employment and quit to pursue a more exciting position with a start-up tech company, Avolo. I was hired as the executive assistant to the young entrepreneur chief executive officer and his much older and more experienced chief operating officer.

The environment was thrilling and the CEO charismatic. He said he was breaking barriers in aviation technology and wanted to grow a new kind of company. Instead of offices, the entire staff of eighty-three people, including the executives, all sat in desk pods in a huge, open office space with no walls.

The company location was next to Boeing's aircraft test field south of Seattle. One entire side of the office space was a wall of windows looking out on the airfield where all day we could see jets taking off and landing. The fast-paced, high energy environment was like gasoline to my already frantic mind.

This was when I met Dylan. He was six-foot, two inches with a strong, wiry build, cropped dark brown hair, and a James Dean "Rebel Without a Cause" look about him. When we went out for the first time, he showed up at my apartment in Redmond, Washington on his lime-green Kawasaki Ninja bullet bike and took me for my first motorcycle ride. We took off like a jet and accelerated to ninety miles per hour.

Electricity shot through my body as I clung tightly to him and squealed, exhilarated. We whizzed up into the mountains, and my breath caught every time we would lean low, speeding around every tight curve in the road.

As I saw how close the asphalt was, a thought popped into my head: *I could just reach out and touch the road!* I squeezed tighter, feeling as though my heart would pound through my rib cage.

We rode for an hour, and when we finally arrived back at my apartment, I was in love with Dylan and motorcycles. He kissed me passionately good night and told me he'd see me the next day. I couldn't sleep that night.

I began spending all of my free time with Dylan. He taught me to ride motorcycles and helped me secure my motorcycle operator's license. I was blissfully happy for a couple months, and then things began to change as he became increasingly emotionally manipulative and unkind.

I didn't recognize what was happening at first because it was subtle. I soon found myself in familiar emotional territory, however, as he began routinely making comments about how he was settling for me because the woman he was in love with wouldn't date him.

During this time, my very organized, introverted roommate became fed up with me because I was staying out late every night and not following the rules she had established for our apartment. She told me it would be best if I moved out.

Dylan suggested instead of moving back in with my parents I should get my own apartment. Becoming isolated from my family again, I was hyper-focused on the motorcycles and relationship with Dylan. That's when I started showing up late for work.

Everything came to a head when I showed up late for work for the third time in a week after a fight with Dylan. That morning, I was fired from my job. The kind, older COO whom I supported could see I was in crisis and offered me a severance to help me out until I could find another job.

I decided what I really needed was a fresh start. In January, I moved to Utah and lived with my aunt and uncle near Salt Lake for a few months. In the past two years, three of my younger sisters had gotten married and one had already had a baby. They were all living in Provo, a city an hour south of Salt Lake, attending Brigham Young University.

I loved being close to them, but being so near made my dream of becoming a wife and a mother feel further away than ever. This prompted me to join an online dating site, where I met a man from a town near Chicago, Illinois.

We had a brief relationship in which he flew me out to visit him at one point, and I visited Chicago for my first time. The relationship became abusive and deteriorated quickly, triggering a depressive episode. I was also struggling because I couldn't find a job in Salt Lake–I had been working for a temp agency since moving there–and I wasn't making any friends. I was lonely and lost.

In May 2001, I decided to move across the country to Chicago, to the consternation of my parents. This move would put me nearly two thousand miles away from my family.

In my mind, the move to a city I had only visited briefly on one occasion–with no job and no contacts–was not only rational, but inspired. To my parents, it was irrational and dangerous. They offered to arrange for me to stay with friends in Chicago if I would agree to begin seeing a therapist–something I continued to resist, even when my doctor recommended it.

Mercifully, a week after arriving, I found an amazing job as an executive assistant to the chief financial officer of an international marketing company.

Two weeks after that, I moved into a studio apartment overlooking Lake Michigan in the Hyde Park neighborhood on the south side near University of Chicago.

Soon after moving in, I kept my promise to my parents and began seeing a therapist for the first time. While she was kind and I enjoyed visiting with her, she was a new, inexperienced therapist, still working on logging enough hours to become fully certified. For my part, I didn't know what I was supposed to talk about. I honestly didn't understand the point of therapy, but I continued to go to please my parents.

I began attending church at a nearby congregation for young single adults and started to make friends. I loved Chicago! It was so vibrant and full of life. That summer I enjoyed attending concerts and festivals near downtown with my new friends.

One morning in late July, I was standing on the train platform on my way to work, and I had an overwhelming feeling of joy and accomplishment. *I am doing it!* I thought happily. *I'm taking care of myself with no one else's help!* I felt a surge of hope that maybe, finally, I had turned a corner.

But the bipolar symptoms had not gone away. A few months into my Chicago adventure, I was sitting in church. Suddenly, I had a sharp pain in my chest that made it hard to breathe. The pain increased, and now I was hyperventilating, trying to get enough oxygen. *Oh my gosh!* I thought in a panic, *I'm having a heart attack!*

I spent eight hours in the emergency room that day while the doctors ran tests and blood work. Sitting alone, I was separated from the rest of the noisy, bustling emergency room by just a curtain, anxiously awaiting my results.

Finally, the doctor came in and took a seat on the little rolling chair next to my bed. With my chart in his hands, he looked at me with a small, patient smile. "I see in your chart you have bipolar disorder," he began.

"Yes," I replied, confused by this unexpected statement.

"Well," he said, pausing for a moment as his eyes flicked down at the chart again. "We've reviewed all of your blood work and scans and can't find anything wrong with you."

"I don't understand. What does that have to do with me having bipolar?" I asked, heat rising in my cheeks.

"I believe what you experienced was an anxiety attack," he explained. "It can feel very much like a heart attack, and even have some similar symptoms like elevated blood pressure and heart rate. But when this happens, there is no physical reason for the symptoms."

I sat there in uncomfortable silence for a few minutes, trying to process what he was telling me. *So does that mean it wasn't real?* My thoughts swirled in disbelief. *But it felt real! I really thought I was going to die! How could that all be in my head?*

"Do you have a psychiatrist?" the ER doctor asked, interrupting my thoughts.

I nodded numbly.

"I recommend you talk to your psychiatrist and see if he or she can give you something to help with your anxiety," he suggested as he quickly signed my discharge papers. Rising from his seat, he handed me the sheet with his recommendation clearly printed on the page and dismissed me.

Obediently, I made an appointment to see my psychiatrist the following week. She was a German woman with a thick accent, short, wiry, wavy gray hair and serious, ice-blue eyes. Her office was small with a dark brown worn leather couch across from her desk. I sat down that late August afternoon and she asked, "What brings you here to see me so urgently?"

I fought back angry tears. "I don't understand what is happening to me!" I exclaimed in frustration. "I have been taking every medication I have been prescribed for the past three and a half years and I am still not better!"

She looked calmly at me, unruffled by my outburst.

"My dear, you are never going to *get better*."

CHAPTER 3

OH, THERE YOU ARE!

I stared open-mouthed at my psychiatrist. Her words spun painfully on repeat around my mind: *"You are never going to get better."* Was that really true?

"Bipolar disorder is a complicated illness for which there is no cure," she informed me in her clinical, detached German intonation. "Sometimes it takes a little while to find the right medications to help manage your disorder effectively. I will write you a prescription for your anxiety that you can take as you need it."

My heart sank as she pulled out her prescription pad and scribbled down yet another drug. I hated my medications already, yet now I had to add a new one.

"In the meantime," she added as she handed me the script, "it would be wise for you to seek help from your therapist to develop some coping skills to address your symptoms."

The best I could manage was to nod meekly as I left her office, feeling dejected and discouraged.

Over the ensuing six months, I began working more diligently with my therapist, hoping desperately to find a way to get a handle on my disorder. Although nothing she suggested seemed to help my bipolar, one conclusion I came to was that marriage was not for me. In the seven years since my divorce, I had consistently gone from one bad relationship to another. The men were either emotionally unavailable or abusive, which were triggers for my mood swings and would send me spiraling again.

I resolved that I would focus on developing a career and be the "cool aunt" to my growing pool of nieces and nephews—no more dating for me. Even though my heart ached for my little girl that I knew was waiting, I believed that some fatal flaw in me only attracted awful men, and I wasn't going to subject her to a father like that. I even canceled my membership to the online dating website.

Life had other plans, however. My membership was still active through the month of September, and one day I received a message from someone interested in my profile. When Scott first contacted me, I told him I wasn't interested in dating, but if he wanted a friend, we could email. I was rather rude to him in the beginning, even getting him mixed up with another man who had messaged me, but Scott wasn't put off. When we first began communicating via email, he asked if I would like to try talking on the phone or instant messaging instead. I said no right away to both and was surprised when he didn't push and was content to continue just emailing. *That never happens with guys!* I thought, incredulous. *Who is he?*

A few weeks after our first contact, I had a particularly rough day at work. I initially tried calling my mom and my sisters, but no one was available. In desperation, I sent Scott an instant message and he responded! For the next half hour, he was goofy and made me laugh, lifting my spirits. After that, we began chatting through instant messenger every afternoon. Two weeks later, I found myself disappointed when our chat session was over. A little nervously I asked if he'd like to talk on the phone later that evening.

He was surprised by my suggestion but readily agreed. That evening we added to our routine with nightly phone conversations. I began to really like him . . . maybe too much.

That's when I knew I needed to pluck up the courage to tell him about my bipolar diagnosis. "Hey, I need to talk to you about something," I began nervously one evening.

"What's up?" he encouraged.

"I . . . I have bipolar disorder," I blurted.

There was silence on the other end of the line for a few moments. Finally, he asked, "So what does that mean? Are you really happy sometimes and then really sad at others?"

"Well . . ." I searched for what to say. "Not really. I have times when my mind races, and I make impulsive decisions, and then other times when I experience really deep depression that makes it hard to function."

Gaining more courage, I told Scott about my history, all about the highs and the lows, about my abusive marriage and other bad relationships. I told him about the jobs I'd lost and all the moves I'd made. When I was finished, there was silence again on the other end of the line. I held my breath, expecting him to say he had to go.

Finally, he spoke. "Wow, I am so sorry you had to go through all of that. That sounds so difficult."

Tears welled up in my eyes as I exhaled and admitted, "Yeah, it really has been."

"So what do you do, take medication?" he asked with sincere curiosity.

We talked late into the night about my treatment, especially the struggles and frustrations I had experienced as I tried to find something to help. When we finally said good night, I worried again that he might not be interested in continuing our friendship.

"So, same time tomorrow?" Scott asked.

I was overcome with gratitude for his kindness and compassion. "Yes! Same time tomorrow!"

We continued growing our friendship through daily emails and phone calls over the following few weeks. Not only was he funny and lighthearted, but he respected my boundaries. I'd never had a man who respected my boundaries! Slowly, I began to trust him.

At Thanksgiving, I flew home to visit my family in Washington. During the trip, I continued to speak each evening with Scott. One night after I got off the phone with him, my father asked with curiosity, "Who was that you were talking with?"

I told him briefly about my friendship with Scott. "Interesting," Dad remarked, looking at me thoughtfully. "This is the first time I have seen you this calm when talking with a man. He sounds like a very kind person."

"He is," I replied, realizing that even though I had yet to meet him, Scott's kindness was what I liked most about him.

When I returned to work on Monday, I was coordinating plans for the company Christmas party scheduled in three weeks. It suddenly occurred to me that the only person I wanted to take was Scott. That night I asked him if he would be willing to be my date to the party.

He said he would agree under one condition. "I want you to meet me in person first and make sure you *really* want me at your company event."

We agreed to meet on December 1, 2001. Scott drove the four and a half hours from his small town in Iowa to spend the day with me. I was so anxious. What if he didn't like me? What if I didn't like him? Was it a mistake to meet in person, let alone go on an official date to the party?

I heard the knock on the door and I nervously opened it. When our eyes met, there was a thrill of recognition. *Oh! There you are!*

He was six-foot, four-inches tall, lean, and strong, with dark brown hair with just a hint of gray coming in on the sides. He had kind, hazel eyes and an easy, impish smile. We had decided to spend the day in Chicago with me playing tour guide. As we drove in his silver Ford Explorer to a parking garage downtown, I felt so joyful and at ease in his company. It was like coming home.

As we exited the parking garage onto Michigan Avenue, however, I began to worry. *What should I do?* I fretted as we walked side by side down the busy street. *I've been telling him I just want to be friends for so long and he's respected that. I really, really like this guy. How do I let him know I want more?*

I was so terrified of rejection that I was afraid to be forward. Still, I needed him to know I had fallen in love with him. As we turned to cross the street, I timidly slid my hand into his and felt a wave of relief and elation wash over me as he squeezed encouragingly.

That was one of the best days of my life. We enjoyed Chicago-style pizza at Pizzeria Due, window-shopped along the Magnificent Mile, and finished up with a movie at my apartment. I didn't want the day to end.

My heart sank as Scott got up to leave and then did a flip-flop when he said apologetically, "I wish I didn't have to go, but it's a long drive home."

He held my hand as we walked slowly to the door. I paused awkwardly. *I want to kiss him so much!* I thought longingly, *but I've already been so forward!*

The space between us felt charged with electricity and then slowly he pulled me in and tenderly kissed me. My heart sang and I wanted to stay in that moment with him forever.

The next two weeks waiting to see him again felt like torture. He rode the train up that time, and after enjoying the Christmas party together, we drove through a rainstorm to Fort Madison, Iowa. That weekend I met his wonderful parents, whom I stayed with, and Scott's sweet six-year-old son, Liam.

Liam was a gentle child with a beautifully active mind. He was a voracious reader, even at that young age. His favorite books were the *Harry Potter* series. He also loved playing video games. I adored a cute quirk he had, that when he ran, he would ball his fists up and hold both arms straight out behind his back. Once I asked him, "Liam, why do you run like that?"

"It makes me run faster!" he declared with enthusiasm. "Just like Sonic the Hedgehog."

I suppressed a laugh as he took off running to demonstrate and my heart swelled with love for this little boy. I was even more delighted when I had the feeling I would be invited into this family. I couldn't believe it. This had been my dream for so long. Could it be real?

We dated long distance for the next few months, talking on the phone during the week and taking turns driving to visit every other weekend. Then in late February, Scott invited me to take a trip to Mexico with him and his brother and sister-in-law. It was a magical week, and every time I saw a church, I would ask him, only half teasing, "Hey, want to get married?"

The more I said it, the more I meant it, and by the end of the week, I wanted more than anything to be his wife. The last night of our trip, we were sitting in the living room of our condo waiting for his brother and sister-in-law to finish getting ready so we could go to dinner. Scott turned to me and asked, "Will you marry me?"

I thought he was joking, like I had been all week, playfully pushing him but not believing the proposal had any significance. Now, however, I caught a meaningful spark in his eyes. "That's not funny," I told Scott.

"I'm being serious," he replied, looking steadily into my eyes. "I was planning to buy a ring this week, but I didn't trust the quality of the ones I saw. The only reason I didn't want to get married here was because I thought it might hurt your parents to not be included."

Stunned for a minute, I finally recovered and responded with enthusiasm, "Yes! Of course I'll marry you!"

I hugged and kissed him, and then he gently pulled me away and said, apologetically, "You can't tell anyone yet because I want you to have a ring first."

I didn't care. I practically floated on air the rest of the trip. One week after we returned, I had a simple, elegant ring on my finger, and it was official.

On April 20, 2002, Scott and I were married in an intimate ceremony surrounded by close family and friends, with Liam standing by Scott. There were blossoms on the trees, birds singing, and the entire world seemed filled with beauty.

Family friends of Scott's surprised us after the ceremony with a carriage ride around the small town. Scott and I brought Liam with us, and I snuggled close to my new husband for warmth against the brisk spring breeze. The steady cadence of the horse plodding along and the rhythm of Scott's heartbeat under my hand caused my chest to swell to the point I thought it might burst! I felt a sense of safety and security with Scott that I had only ever felt with my father.

Two weeks after we were married, Scott and I were in the car driving to the department of motor vehicles to get my new driver's license. When we arrived, I was finishing getting ready so Scott pulled into a parking spot and turned off the car. As I looked in the mirror to touch up my makeup, I could feel Scott's eyes on me and I experienced a moment of familiar apprehension.

Glancing over at him, I asked, "Why are you looking at me like that?"

He smiled lovingly and replied, "You are so gorgeous. I can't believe you're mine!"

My entire body relaxed, then warmed with love and gratitude. I leaned over and kissed him. He really was the man I had been praying and waiting for my entire life.

CHAPTER 4

I JUST WANT TO BE A GOOD MOM!

The first step in my new life together with my husband was a big move. There was a major culture shock going from Chicago with a population of nearly three million to rural Fort Madison, Iowa with only ten thousand. I fell in love with small town living quickly, though, and I couldn't wait to come home each day to my little family.

We lived on a quiet residential street in a one-hundred-year-old, two-bedroom farmhouse that Scott owned before we were married, and I adored it. I quickly went to work giving it a "woman's touch" by repainting and adding curtains—I was so excited to have my own home! Liam attended an elementary school across the street, and Scott and I arranged our work schedules so that one of us was always home when Liam was.

I was in heaven being a stepmom. I delighted in arranging activities for Liam and his friends, we rode bikes together to the library, and I loved having him teach me how to play video games. We had fun as a family attending the frequent parades in "downtown" Fort Madison, and I spent weeks planning my stepson's August birthday party, as well as making his Halloween costume in October.

The mood swings were manageable at first. It was an adjustment being married again and trying to deal with new stressors, but Scott was patient. My new psychiatrist, Dr. Davies, was determined that we could find a combination of medications that would help me stabilize.

In November, Scott and I decided we wanted to try getting pregnant. It was something we knew we had to plan because three of the four prescriptions I was taking could cause birth defects. I made an appointment with my psychiatrist and began the process of titrating off my drugs.

The excitement I felt at finally trying to have a baby initially outweighed my apprehension about going off of my meds. I spent hours dreaming of meeting my little girl who had spoken to me and had saved me years prior. In late February, however, I began to have misgivings as I felt myself sliding deeper and deeper into the gloom of an overwhelming depression.

One day I was driving to work, having barely won the battle with the darkness that morning. I felt like I was moving through tar; each action I took, from getting out of bed to brushing my teeth and getting dressed required a herculean effort. I kept crying off and on during the thirty-minute drive, and when I arrived, I called my obstetrician to make an emergency appointment.

Upon entering her office, I was asked to give a urine sample before being escorted to the examination room. When the doctor entered, I explained to her that I couldn't handle being off of my medications, and I needed to have her put me back on birth control–and give my psychiatrist the go-ahead to start me back on my meds.

She assured me that she could accommodate that as soon as the results were back on my pregnancy test confirming that I wasn't pregnant.

Ten minutes later, a nurse came into the exam room and asked me to follow her. "The doctor would like to speak with you in her office," she explained.

Confused and disconcerted by this unexpected request, I followed her down the hall. Upon entering the small, cozy room I found my obstetrician seated behind a large wooden desk.

"Take a seat," she said kindly, gesturing to the chairs opposite her desk.

I sat down apprehensively and looked to her for an explanation. *This is the kind of thing I see in movies when people hear they have cancer*, I thought as my chest began to constrict.

"You won't be able to go back on your medications," she began, "because you are pregnant."

I sat there for a moment without speaking. "Could you say that again?" I asked, not sure I had heard her correctly.

"You're pregnant, Michelle," she repeated.

Again, I just looked at her and then tears began to roll down my cheeks and I asked unsteadily, "Could I please use your phone to call my husband?"

"Of course!" she replied, turning her desk phone around to face me.

In a daze, I dialed Scott's work number. As I listened to the ring of the phone, questions began rolling around my head with a mixture of joy and worry, *Do I finally get to meet my little girl? Can I handle pregnancy?*

"Hello?" I heard his voice on the other end of the line.

"Scott? I'm pregnant," I blurted.

"What? No, you're not," he said, clearly caught off guard by the unexpected announcement.

"Yes, I am!" I reasserted, tears now flowing freely down my face.

After a moment of silence, he asked, "How can you be sure?"

"I'm sitting in the doctor's office right now," I responded adamantly. "Do you want to talk with her?"

The doctor smiled warmly at me, clearly enjoying the exchange.

After another brief pause, Scott said, "Well, there's no going back now, is there?" I could hear a mixture of excitement and uncertainty in his voice.

"Are you happy?" I asked, worried about how he would respond.

"Of course I am!" he said, this time without hesitation. "And I already have a name picked out."

Relief flooded through me, warming my heart and my soul. I already knew Scott was a wonderful father. *We can do this together!* I thought, *I'm not alone.*

And so it was that we embarked on a nine-month rollercoaster with a mixture of anxiety and joyful anticipation. On the evening of October 22, 2003, a week before my due date, I was on the phone with my mother when I felt an intense cramping in my abdomen.

"Hang on a second," I gasped in surprise.

"Michelle? Are you okay?" my mother asked with concern.

After a few moments, I recovered and replied, "I'm fine. I've been having really bad cramps this afternoon."

"You're in labor!" she exclaimed with enthusiasm.

"No, Mom, it's just cramps," I insisted.

That's when my mother, who had given birth ten times, patiently explained, "Sweetheart, that's what labor feels like."

The next twenty-four hours were rough. I had read lots of books about childbirth, but having never experienced it before, I felt woefully unprepared. Labor lasted for over twenty-six hours. In the end, I pushed for over two hours and started to become convinced that the baby was never coming out.

And then, suddenly, she arrived!

I watched the nurse ask Scott if he would like to cut the umbilical cord. Reaching out for my baby daughter as she cried in protest, I mused in wonderment, "Wow, she has so much hair!"

As the nurse laid her on my chest, she calmed almost instantly. Gazing into the little pink face of my Gabrielle for the first time, I thought, *Oh, there you are!* That beautiful sense of familiarity I felt when I first met Scott reflected once more, this time from my newborn daughter's eyes back at me.

Scott brought Liam to the hospital later to meet baby Gabby. He shyly approached and held out a little stuffed cat he had purchased in the gift shop for her.

"Would you like to hold your little sister?" I asked him, gently.

He nodded with a smile and I invited him to sit in the chair by my bed while Scott brought Gabby over and placed her in Liam's arms.

In that moment, the world was perfect, whole, and complete.

The first couple months after my daughter was born were equally blissful. Every day I loved looking into her eyes and witnessing the beginnings of her toothless grin. I quit my job so I could be a full-time mother.

Unfortunately, in the beginning of the third month after she was born, I could feel myself spiraling helplessly fast into depression. I started to feel detached emotionally from my little girl and struggled to get out of bed. I called Dr. Davies one day crying, and he told me I would need to stop breastfeeding immediately and go back on my medications.

The next week was torturous. Gabby didn't like the formula or bottle and cried constantly. I was in pain from being engorged and slogging through the depths of an emotionally bottomless pit. *How can I hold a precious little creature that has filled me with such joy and at the same time feel like I am being consumed with darkness?* I didn't know a thing about postpartum depression, and so it didn't make a lick of sense.

Every night when I went to bed, I poured out my heart to God in prayer. "Heavenly Father, please help me! My little girl is finally here . . . and I'm failing her!" I wouldn't give up, though; I would keep fighting. There had to be a way! I just desperately wanted God to throw me a lifeline so I could be the mother I always wanted to be for my little girl.

Six months postpartum, I began experiencing unexpected physical symptoms—dizziness, blackouts, and rapid, excessive weight loss and hair loss. When I sought an explanation from my obstetrician, she told me not to worry. Just switch to more calorie-dense foods, she suggested, and my body would eventually balance out. Those symptoms lasted six months before they finally abated.

That next year was a mixture of joyful firsts and painful struggles. I loved my little girl with all my heart, but I was plagued with a persistently deteriorating mental state.

"It's like the medications sometimes take the edge off, but the storm is still raging!" I exclaimed in exasperation to my doctor one day. "And the side effects are unbearable."

Dr. Davies was a short, heavyset man in his late fifties. He reminded me of Gimli the dwarf from the *Lord of the Rings* movies in both looks (albeit with shorter hair and beard), and the sound of his robust, gravelly voice. He used a motorized scooter to get around due to health issues.

This doctor was actually kind to me. He took his time in our visits, unlike my previous doctors, and listened with patience to my concerns. "We're on the right track," he reassured me with confidence. "It can take some people longer than others to find the right combination of medications."

I prayed he was right. *Okay*, I said to myself, hanging on with hope, *I just need to be patient until we find the right meds, I guess.* Fortunately, I went through periods when I was a fun, exciting mom. I would start big projects, like making elaborate costumes for Liam and Gabby or planning involved "themed" parties, staying up late into the night, filled with unbounded energy.

When the high was gone, however, I would crash for days and spend hours and hours in front of the television while the dishes and laundry piled up, and we ate takeout because I wasn't grocery shopping.

When Gabby was two years old, I was hired as head coach for the local YMCA swim team. I was so excited about the new position and loved sharing my passion for swimming with the children and youth in the community. I even had the opportunity to help some adult triathletes in our town improve their swimming technique and skill.

Unfortunately, my anxiety attacks grew worse. I started having terrible bouts of nausea and even visual distortions, making it frequently necessary to leave practice early.

My assistant coach was a parent of one of the swimmers. She offered to cover for me when I was "unwell." She reassured me that I was a wonderful coach and she wanted me to continue training her daughter. I was grateful for her help, but discouraged that I needed it at all.

Scott continued to be supportive and patient, but he worked long hours as a supervisor at a local manufacturing plant, which kept him away more than either of us liked.

Our son, Marcus, was born June 29, 2006. He was a chunky little baby with iridescent blonde hair and chubby pink cheeks. The first night in the hospital after he was born, I was lying in bed in the quiet of the room, listening to my little boy breathing peacefully as he slept. As I connected with the little guy's strong spirit, I was unexpectedly overcome with an intense desire to call Scott, Liam, and little two-year-old Gabby and tell each one how much I loved them!

I looked in wonder at the cherubic figure in the plastic hospital bassinet and realized that he had increased my capacity for love; not just for him, but for everyone else in my life! As I related the experience to Scott the next day, I shared in wonder, "It was like the moment in Dr. Suess's book, *The Grinch Who Stole Christmas*, when the Grinch's heart grows three sizes!"

Following Marcus's birth, I experienced the same joyful three months before my condition began to deteriorate rapidly . . . *again*. I resumed taking medication. Three months later, the dizziness, blackouts, weight loss, and hair loss recurred with greater severity. I was twenty-five pounds lighter than my lowest pre-pregnancy weight—you could see my ribs and I looked anorexic even though I was eating constantly. I passed out on the deck one night at swim practice, and the hair loss was so great that when I rubbed my scalp it felt like I'd shaved my head from the regrowth.

My obstetrician referred me this time to an endocrinologist and I was diagnosed with postpartum hyperthyroidism. "This should self-correct in the next year," the doctor reassured me.

"Could this possibly be caused by my bipolar medications?" I asked, thinking about the correlation between the timing of restarting my meds, the three months of it building back up in my system, and the onset of the hyper-thyroidism symptoms.

"I strongly doubt it," the doctor replied with authority. "There is no reason to believe there is any connection between your medication and the condition. This is simply how your body reacts to the postpartum hormone changes."

I wasn't sure if I believed him, but he was the one who had gone to medical school, and I had nothing but my gut feeling to prove otherwise. That's why I took what he said next to heart.

"I would strongly urge you not to have any more children," he warned. "If you do, it will undoubtedly destroy your thyroid."

Shortly after Marcus was born, Scott started a two-year executive MBA program at the University of Iowa–something I encouraged him to pursue–in addition to working full-time at the plant.

It was during this time that I began to experience a horrible new symptom: uncontrollable rage. Though I couldn't remember anything leading up to the incident, I found myself screaming at the top of my lungs into the face of my little boy as he started to cry, eyes wide in terror. I couldn't see straight and I started to dissociate. I felt like I was having an out-of-body experience, watching myself rage at my child. When it was over and I could gain control again, I ran to my room and sobbed.

That night was the first time I had a nightmare about dying. The vivid nightmares became more and more frequent over the following months and I would wake up in the morning feeling panicked.

When those awful dreams weren't plaguing me, I experienced insomnia. Those torturous nights, I lay in bed exhausted and wide awake. "Heavenly Father, PLEASE let me sleep!" I begged. My mind was like a dryer filled with shoes rolling around and around, pounding inside my brain.

I shouldn't have yelled at my kids like that. Why can't I be a good mom? Scott didn't sign on for this! He would be better off with a different wife. Why do I keep spending money and getting us in debt? It's humiliating that I can't stop!

Around and around and around . . . until finally:

Heavenly Father, PLEASE LET ME SLEEP!

Throughout all of this, I was faithfully going to my psychiatric appointments and dutifully taking my medication. I struggled with most prescriptions because the side effects were intolerable, so my doctor simply started adding drugs on top of each other to mitigate side effects.

At one point, I was on seven different medications and I felt like a zombie. Sure, I didn't cry at the drop of a hat, but feeling nothing was worse than feeling everything. I captured my growing hopelessness when writing in my journal:

December 5, 2007
   Gabby is always asking me, "Are you happy, Mommy?" She should have a happy mother–she deserves a good, loving, patient mom.

The terrible, incessant nightmares progressed to daydreams. Random scenarios would pop into my head of ways I could die. At first I was horrified by the thoughts and wouldn't tell anyone, afraid they would put me in the hospital. Then, gradually, I began finding relief in the idea of dying, convinced that everyone would be better off if I were gone.

One day in March of 2008, I was driving along a road next to the Mississippi River with my children. They were watching *Finding Nemo* on the overhead DVD player in the back of the van. I suddenly became gripped with an overpowering urge to drive into the river. *I can't hurt my children!* I thought in desperation and fear. Silent tears rolled down my cheeks as I fought an internal war.

I called my sister, begging for help. She stayed on the phone with me until I was safe at home and then spoke with Scott about what had happened. He was leaving in two days to fly to Brazil as part of his final project for his master's program. Concerned about leaving me alone, they decided to have me fly out to Utah with my children so she could care for me until he returned.

When we arrived at the Salt Lake City airport, my mother, who had flown out to Utah from Washington to help my sister take care of me and my children, arrived to pick us up.

She was shocked when she saw the state I was in. I was emaciated, meek, and fragile, and kept repeating quietly, "I just want to be a good mom, I just want to be a good mom."

"It was heartrending," she shared later.

I was taken to the psychiatric wing at the University of Utah hospital, where I was admitted to the locked ward. I spent a week there while the doctors evaluated me. They determined that the best course of action was electroconvulsive therapy—otherwise known as shock therapy.

I sat in the consultation room, trying to focus on what the doctor was saying through the fog in my head.

"Your brain is like a computer that has been frozen and we need to reboot it," she explained in a clinical tone.

"I don't understand. How will you do that?" I asked, my body filled with apprehension.

"We will initiate controlled seizures in your brain three times a week for the next four weeks," she clarified. "This can disrupt your short-term memory so you will need to do things like read a book with a plot and keep a journal to help your brain reconnect between sessions."

I wasn't sure how I was supposed to remember to read a book or write in my journal if my memory was being damaged, but I had to trust the doctor because I didn't know what else to do—I was beyond wit's end. The problem is that the damage to my memory ended up being more permanent than the doctor had eluded to and most of my "memories" from that time period are based on what others have shared with me—and my sporadic journal entries.

Due to a shortage of beds, the hospital released me into the care of my family while I began the ECT treatments. However, following the third treatment, I experienced a psychotic episode. I ranted incoherently and became violent and threatening—not my nature. My brother-in-law had to physically restrain me to prevent me from harming myself or someone else.

"You had a hollow, vacant look in your eyes," my sister later recounted. "I couldn't see my sister there . . . and it was terrifying."

I was readmitted to the hospital for what would be the final three weeks of the treatment.

When my husband returned from Brazil two weeks after I arrived in Utah, he came out to help and was horrified by what he saw. Because he had been out of the country, he had not known about the second hospitalization, nor those ECT treatments.

Later he told me, "The hospital let me take you out for the afternoon, and when you walked into the lobby, I barely recognized you," he explained, clearly uncomfortable with the memory. "Your makeup was dramatically different, with heavy black eyeliner around your eyes, and you were even dressed differently." He shared how I had rambled on about how I was going to get rich with my direct marketing business and insisted we test drive Audis because we were going to buy them soon.

Disturbed by his first time witnessing this fully manic version of his wife, Scott drove me back to the hospital. After checking me back in, he asked to speak to the doctor. She assured him that my treatment protocol was appropriate and necessary, and that he should just go home. Unable to do anything for me and needing to return to work, Scott took the kids back to Iowa the next day.

Two weeks later, the doctor changed my diagnosis to "bipolar one" and insisted that I start lithium before she would release me.

"Please don't put me on that medication!" I pleaded. "I took that ten years ago and I had a psychotic episode." I shuddered as I recalled the *Pop* . . . *Fizz* . . . sensation in my brain.

"That would not have been caused by the lithium," she insisted, "but an unrelated psychotic episode."

"But I don't have a history of psychosis!" I exclaimed in frustration.

"Well, that's not true, now, is it?" she said, looking intently at me. "We've witnessed psychosis this past week. It clearly just wasn't *caught* earlier."

I sat there, feeling helpless and trapped. I had been separated from my husband and children for five weeks and I just wanted to go home.

"This is the most effective treatment for bipolar and you need to take it if you don't want to end up back here again," the doctor said with finality.

I was completely defeated. *I just want to be a good mother,* came my ever present mantra.

"Okay," I said, surrendering submissively.

I was released the next day with my prescription for lithium. I flew home to Iowa. Two days later, I made the first of two attempts on my life, which landed me back in the hospital—this time in Iowa City, Iowa.

Two days after arriving, I told the psychiatrist that I wanted to go home. "That won't be possible," he responded, "you're having a reaction to the medication you're taking and we need to keep you here until we can get you stable."

"No! I don't want to be here anymore!" I cried out through angry tears. "I've been separated from my family for a month and a half and I want to go home!"

He shook his head, and that made me even more angry. I squared my shoulders.

"I checked myself in, and I will check myself out," I insisted adamantly.

"I'm sorry," the doctor responded, "but that is not an option. If you try to leave, we will have you committed."

I stared mutely at him as his words sank in. I had come seeking help and relief and found instead a prison.

Ironically, at the end of the week, my symptoms had not improved much, but I was released because my insurance would not approve a longer stay.

Less than a week later, I was admitted again to a psychiatric ward after a third attempt on my life. This time it was at our local hospital. The treating psychiatrist was Dr. Davies. He was horrified when he learned what I'd been through and put in my file that I was allergic to lithium to prevent any doctor from ever prescribing it to me again.

PART 2
STEPS TO HEALING

CHAPTER 5

STEP ONE-MOOD CYCLE SURVIVAL GUIDE:
A Lifeboat in the Bipolar Storm

A couple of weeks after I was released from my third hospitalization, I kept trying to get back to "normal." One day, I went to the bank to deposit a check. Panic filled me as I stood frozen in front of the bank teller, my pen stuck halfway through my signature on the check. *Oh my gosh! I can't remember how to sign my own name!* Cheeks hot with mortification, I felt many pairs of eyes on me.

What if they think I'm forging my signature? I worried, desperately searching my memory for what I was supposed to do next.

Dropping the pen and grabbing the check, I mumbled quickly, "I'm so sorry, I forgot something. . ."

With my head down, I hurried past the growing line behind me and back out to my car. I couldn't believe I would have to ask Scott to endorse and deposit the check for me. What a stupid thing to have to ask for help with! Getting into the driver's seat, I let out a shaky breath.

Since my release from the hospital, I hadn't been doing well. My mood swings were more extreme and frequent than ever before. Some days I felt overwhelming love for my husband, and other days I was certain I needed to leave him. Every day there was a new compulsion—get a tattoo, start a business, get on a bus and go anywhere . . . but here.

It didn't help one bit that those electroconvulsive therapy treatments had badly damaged my memory. Just yesterday I had been talking to my mom on the phone about plans for Marcus's upcoming birthday and I mentioned his birth date. There was a pause and then my mom said, "Michelle, that's your dad's birthday." She was right. As I searched my mind for my son's birth date, I couldn't find it. And now today, I had been humiliated at the bank when I couldn't remember how to sign my own name!

The next day, I stood in the kitchen doing the dishes with the May sunshine filling the room. I could hear Gabby and Marcus playing make-believe in the other room. *How does that sun keep shining?* I thought miserably. Every day, I was trapped in the middle of a stormy ocean. Whenever I gasped for air, another wave crashed down on me. I was exhausted. Mustering my strength, I went into the living room to see what the kids were up to.

Little four-year-old Gabby was wearing the golden Belle princess dress I had made for her the prior Halloween. She danced around and happened to stop in front of the window where the sun shining on her messy blonde curls created a halo around her head. She had squeezed chubby two-year-old Marcus into last year's lion costume and was giggling delightedly as he roared at her.

At that moment, I heard a voice clearly inside of me. It didn't sound like the fiends and liars in my head that relentlessly barraged me with dark thoughts of death. This one filled my mind and my heart. It was calm, quiet, and firm.

If you ever succeed in ending your life, you will ruin hers. She will believe it was her fault and it will ruin her life.

Sitting there, I was stunned. I had believed with every fiber of my being that my husband and children would be better off without me. As tears filled my eyes, I knew that the words were true—I would ruin Gabby's life if I ended mine.

But how can I keep living when there is no hope for ever getting better? I agonized.

It didn't matter. I would do anything for my daughter, including living through the pain of persistent mental illness. Even if my life had no value, hers did. A growing resolve filled my heart.

I will survive for her, I thought with determination.

Gabby looked up at me and noticed my wet cheeks. "Are you sad, Mommy?" she asked, concern and worry in her little voice.

"Oh sweetie, Mommy's okay," I said, meeting her serious blue eyes. "I just missed you so much while I was gone."

She came over to me and tenderly wrapped her small arms around my neck and kissed my cheek. "I'll help you, Mommy," she said sweetly.

I hugged her tightly. She had no idea that she already had.

From that moment, my purpose seemed very clear: even if all I could do was learn to *suffer well with my bipolar*, I would do it. When those intrusive, dark thoughts came, I would ask for help, no matter how humiliating it was.

For two more years, I did survive. I suffered as well as I could. I continued to struggle with mood swings, sometimes barely hanging on by my fingernails. One day in April 2010, however, I couldn't get my head above the surface and the dark voices returned, trying to convince me that death was the only way out. I kept my promise to my daughter in my heart, and submissively returned to the hospital; I had an incentive to keep fighting that trumped all the pain.

After a week in that psychiatric ward, I returned home. I sat outside in the spring sunshine watching my children play in the yard and noticed that the hyacinth, our "anniversary flowers," had popped up out of the thawing earth.

A smile crossed my face as I remembered that my father had planted some of these flowers that had decorated the tables at our wedding luncheon in our yard. That was eight years prior, and every year since then they had bloomed in April. I was struck by how resilient those little bulbs were. We'd had an extremely hard winter and still, without fail, they bloomed.

As I sat there looking at the perennial survivors, I had the very logical thought, *No one is coming to save me. I need to save myself.* At that moment, the image of a lifeboat entered my mind.

Was there a lifeboat I could use to help me weather my perpetual storm? Was there a way to start managing my mood swings so I didn't go under completely?

There has to be a way to build a lifeboat for myself! I thought resolutely. *The storm isn't a surprise anymore, so there must be a way to prepare for and weather it.*

I went into the house and retrieved my journal and pen. Returning, I sat with my face to the sun, my children playing happily nearby, and began to write down what I thought I needed to steadily keep my head above the water. Over the following few years, those notes and that learned–and earned–wisdom developed into my Mood Cycle Survival Guide. It became my lifeboat for the times when my bipolar symptoms raged.

Over the next ten years, I used this guide to successfully manage my bipolar mood swings. It didn't eliminate the storms, but it kept me afloat and I never had to return to the hospital.

By choosing to manage the symptoms proactively, I discovered that I could minimize the impact on myself and my family and even shorten the duration of the mood swings. It was also empowering to realize that I had more resources at my disposal than I had ever understood, both within me and surrounding me. This survival guide became my safety net as I moved along the path toward healing.

Mood Cycle Survival Guide

Mood swings and bipolar symptoms can make you feel helpless. It feels like something happening to you that you have no control over. Your Mood Cycle Survival Guide will help you change that dynamic. It will help you to proactively manage your bipolar episodes instead of being victimized by them.

The Mood Cycle Survival Guide has four steps:

Step One: Response Team
Step Two: Early Warning System
Step Three: Power Priorities
Step Four: Rebooting the System

Remember, this guide is a living document, meaning it will evolve over time as you use it and find what works and what doesn't. I do promise that, as you work diligently to develop and consistently use your guide and with the examples you've just experienced through my journey, you will find your strength. Soon, you will keep your head above the water, too, and (I dare say), sail above the storm more victoriously in your own lifeboat.

Step One: Response Team

Each of us has at least one person (sometimes many people), in our lives who care about our well-being and are willing to help when we are facing challenges. The problem is that if we live in a perpetual state of emergency and don't acknowledge any responsibility for those emergencies, we can exhaust those resources. It can strain or do serious damage to relationships, sometimes even destroy them.

The value of identifying your Response Team ahead of time is that you are acknowledging the need for help, working with your team to clarify what they are willing to do, and how you can ask for their help when you need it. This establishes important boundaries and shows respect for these vital people. Be mindful not to stress those resources beyond the agreed upon limits.

Here are the key people to identify for your Response Team:

1. **Psychiatrist and/or therapist.** When you experience bipolar symptoms, especially if there are any thoughts of self-harm or harm to others, you need to address these with your mental health professional immediately. It is crucial to discuss how to reach them and what your plan will be if you begin to struggle with emotional instability.
2. **Spouse or significant other.** If you are married or in a committed relationship, it is critical that your partner is part of your Response Team. It is not fair or healthy for either of you (or for your relationship itself), to expect your partner to simply deal with the consequences of your disorder, with no defined role in the solution.
   Note: If your partner is willing, it can be very helpful to work through this part of the plan with the assistance of a mental health professional. An objective, professional perspective can assist you both, making sure that you are still maintaining healthy boundaries that can preserve and even strengthen your relationship significantly.
3. **Support for your children.** If you have children, it will be key to identify a few people who you trust to be part of your team to watch over them during emergencies. Speak to these chosen adults and ask them how they would be willing and able to help. It is extremely important to limit what help you ask of them. This should be temporary, limited

51

assistance so that you don't put too great a strain on the relationship, or on them and their own families. This ensures you can count on them when you truly need them.

4. **Employer support**. If you work, discuss your needs with your employer. Together, you can identify a strategy that includes what your needs are and what accommodations your employer might be willing to make, enabling you to show up professionally and still get the help you need. Nowadays, many more people in the workplace understand and respect mental health, and there is growing support for additional resources at work and at home.

5. **Other potential needed support**. Identify any other areas–church, school, volunteer positions, etc.–where commitment and support should be discussed in advance. While this can feel hard, I promise you it is a vital step and provides bandwidth when you need it.

6. **Community Resources.** Identify resources available in your community for mental health support. These may include:
   ◦ Addiction recovery groups
   ◦ Crisis hotlines
   ◦ Mental health support groups and more

Include these in your guide so they are readily accessible to you. Keep these resources handy in your phone as well.

Step Two: Early Warning System

Early warning systems are set up in many areas of the world where severe weather or significant seismic activity could potentially cause disasters. It gives response teams an opportunity to prepare and have resources in place to save anyone in crisis more effectively.

Creating an Early Warning System for identifying bipolar symptoms in advance enables you to be *proactive* rather than *reactive* in managing your mood swings. Here are four resources that will help you become more self-aware and better able to recognize your symptoms so you can begin addressing them more quickly.

1. **Utilize a mood-tracking app.** Become an expert on yourself. Use a mood-tracking app to look for symptoms, patterns, and triggers. My favorite app is *Bearable*. There is a free version and a paid version. (The paid version is very inexpensive and the company often offers discounts.) This tool in particular is very useful because it is simple to use and highly customizable to you and your needs.

2. **Ask for input from those who know you best.** You can ask your partner and other close friends or relatives what they observe when you experience symptoms. It is important to have a trusting, healthy relationship with the people you ask for input. As I mentioned, this can be very vulnerable, but ultimately empowering.

3. **Identify "triggers" and "red flags."** *Triggers* are interactions or situations that provoke symptoms. In my case, new relationships and moving were both triggers that brought on mood swings. *Red flags* are symptoms that indicate an impending depressive or manic state. Some of my red flags were sleeplessness and racing thoughts for mania, and fatigue and muddy thinking for depression. The more expert you become at recognizing these warning signs early, the more proactive you can become at managing them.

4. **Be a "team player."** When I first asked my husband for feedback on my mental state, I discovered it was hard for me to hear it. He would indicate that he saw certain symptoms or red flags and often I would get upset or angry at him for speaking about them. This made him less willing to share his observations with me—to him, it felt like a trap.

Once Scott told me he was worried that my rapid and animated explanation about a new plan I had to reupholster some furniture might be a red flag that I was getting hypomanic and I blew up at him. Later, after I calmed down, I was able to realize that I felt like he was saying I was broken, and it hurt. I knew my husband loved me and was just trying to help; after all, it was me who had asked him to tell me when he saw red flags.

We have since come up with a way for him to approach me so that he knows what to say and I agree to listen to him with an open mind. I recognized that for this to work, I had to be a team player. It did no good for me to get angry about what was happening to me.

Again, this is a very vulnerable position to be in with your partner. In order for it to be productive and safe, it is important to have a trusting, healthy relationship.

Having an Early Warning System allows you and your team to respond more quickly and effectively. You will be empowered to respond proactively rather than reactively when you experience symptoms.

Step Three: Power Priorities

One of my biggest struggles when I was experiencing both manic and depressed states was meeting basic needs for both me and my family. When I was going through mania, I would become hyper-focused on huge projects, neglecting basic needs like eating and by extension feeding my children. When I was depressed, I struggled to get out of bed and do basic self-care. In both situations, things that mattered most were getting neglected.

A couple of years into working on this guide, our family was living in Ohio and experienced a five-day power outage due to ice storms. Like many families around us, we were unprepared and really suffered. At one point, we were invited to a neighbor's home who had a power generator. Thanks to them, we were able to enjoy heat, warm food, and warm showers. I was struck by the fact that the generator was not able to power the entire home, so our neighbors determined their "power priorities"---the needs that mattered most until the main power came back online.

That experience helped me recognize that I needed to do the same thing for myself when my bipolar storms threw my emotional and mental power offline. Here are a few ways you can discover those priorities in your life.

1. **Identify all responsibilities.** This is important because your mind constantly reminds you of the things it thinks you *should be* doing. In a manic state, this can ramp you up further, and in a depressed state it can make you feel worse. Be certain to include things that you expect of yourself, like spending time with your children doing activities and outings, personal care routines, exercise, etc. Also include what you

believe others expect of you, including church, school, social or family obligations, and more.

NOTE: Trying to catalog your responsibilities all at once may likely create anxiety and can cause you to lose the motivation to complete this important task. Instead, take your time creating this list to be kind to yourself. This first step is important.

2. **Determine your priorities.** This can feel impossible sometimes because you may feel like *everything* is important. But remember the generator; under emergency situations, you cannot keep everything running. Keep this list of priorities very small.

   See the following graphic for an example of how to do this task. On the left, a full list of everything from step one, on the right will be your Power Priorities in each category: (i.e. "self-care," "children," "home"). For example, if your full list is fifteen items long, your Power Priorities list should only contain three or four items.

   (Refer to the graphic on the next page.)

   The two things that helped me the most in this process were first, recognizing that my primary responsibilities for my emotional resources are myself, my husband, and my children. If I have limited emotional resources, they get first dibs! If there is nothing left for anyone else, that is okay. Your primary responsibilities may differ, especially if you are not married or have children. Clearly identify what your primary responsibilities are–your first is yourself–and then choose your Power Priorities based on those needs.

   Second, identify your personal boundaries. I realized that I was only truly responsible *for* myself and *to* my immediate family. I identified things and people who were using up the emotional resources that I needed to care for myself and my family. I called them "resource vampires" and learned to "just say no."

3. **Make Your Plan.** Just as the electrician wired the generator into the priority power needs ahead of the storm, you need to make your auxiliary power plan ahead of time. When your emotional power goes out, refer to your guide so you will know exactly what you need to do each day and what you are going to let go of until your power is back online.

Self-Care	Self-Care
FULL LIST	**POWER PRIORITIES**
Take micronutrients	Take micronutrients
Yoga	Grounding/Restorative yoga
Run	---
Mindfulness Meditation	---
Journaling	---
Read scriptures	Listen to scriptures
Shower/ Get dressed	Shower/get dressed
Put on Makeup	---
Blow-dry and Fix hair	---

Home	Home
FULL LIST	**POWER PRIORITIES**
Yardwork	---
Laundry	Laundry
Dishes	Dishes
Tidy House	---
Bathrooms	---
Vacuum	---
Sweep/Mop floors	---
Clean Windows	---
Cook Full Meals	---
Meal Planning	Simple Meals (pre planned meal plan)
Grocery Shopping	---

Your plan should include two parts:

Part one identifies your Power Priorities, which might include a schedule for what your day would look like. These Power Priorities should be *very minimal*. If you have the energy to do more, you can, but keep the plan simple so it is sustainable. Then, I suggest you rejoice in your minimal accomplishments and express gratitude for having had sufficient energy to accomplish those tasks.

Part two of your plan is how to let others know that you are unable to meet obligations that didn't make the list. For example, when I am severely depressed, I let my church leaders know that I am not able to help with church functions. Sometimes, if I can, I will help delegate while I am not feeling well. It is important to let people know ahead of time that this is a possibility so it doesn't hit them broadside when it happens. Remember, you are setting a boundary, not asking for their permission. Otherwise, you may feel "guilty" for "letting people down" and thus drain your metaphorical generator needlessly.

Step Four: Rebooting the System

When there is a storm or disaster that causes the power to go out, the power company has procedures in place to restore power to the affected areas. They first have to identify the cause of the outage—downed power lines or blown transformers. Then they go to work to repair the damage so they can get the power back up and running.

Similarly, it is important that you have a plan in place to get your emotional and mental power back online. If you identify this process ahead of time, it will help you to see your way forward and follow your plan so that you don't get mired down in your emotional struggles.

1. **Adjustments to medications or micronutrients.** The very first thing that you need to determine is if the medication or micronutrients you are taking need to be adjusted. If you are taking medication, this will require a trip to your psychiatrist or possibly a hospitalization if you are a danger to yourself or others. Contact your psychiatrist's office

right away to determine which is the best course of action based on the severity of your symptoms. Don't be afraid to ask important questions and be an advocate for yourself.

If you, like me, are using micronutrients (small doses of vitamins and minerals vital to our human bodies), then contact whoever is helping you to get assistance adjusting your supplements. There are a number of different factors that can alter your supplemental needs. It is essential to seek guidance from someone with specialized education in this area to help you get the nutritional support your brain and body need to get back in balance. (This will be explained in more detail in chapter 6.)

2. **Identify and resolve triggers.** Anyone who suffers with bipolar experiences triggers. As you use your Mood Cycle Survival Guide, allow yourself to recognize what may have triggered your symptoms at this time. This is accomplished through using your Early Warning System in Step Two. You can then work with a therapist to determine if there are triggers that can be resolved through therapy or eliminated through boundaries. (Therapy will be discussed in more detail in Chapter 7.)

   It is important to identify emotional triggers and outside stressors that contribute to or cause symptoms so you can learn to better manage your emotional health. This process can be extremely empowering as you focus on becoming more self-aware instead of embarrassed. Self-knowledge is power.

3. **Self-care routine.** It is important to work on developing a self-care routine that includes mindfulness meditation and some form of emotionally restorative exercise or yoga. This helps your body and mind to become healthier and aid in your resilience during, and while recovering from, your mood swings. This part of your plan will evolve and develop as you go through the steps to healing in the following chapters.

Writing out and implementing your Mood Cycle Survival Guide is foundational to your success in healing your bipolar. Healing takes time and you will continue to experience symptoms along the way. Utilizing a Mood Cycle Survival Guide will help you become *proactive* in managing your symptoms and mood swings, lessening the impact on you and your family and shortening the duration of the symptoms so you can keep moving toward healing.

To get a free program to create your Mood Cycle Survival Guide that includes videos, lessons, and a workbook go to: www.theupsideofbipolar.com/free/

CHAPTER 6

STEP TWO-MICRONUTRIENTS:
Waking Up

D r. Davies sat at his cluttered desk and skimmed through the pile of information I had just handed him. Anxious to hear his thoughts, I shivered involuntarily. His office was always cold and my skin was covered in a thin layer of sweat from the intense Midwest summer heat and humidity.

It was mid-August 2010, and my friend Peggy, who also suffered from bipolar disorder, had told me about a micronutrient treatment called EMPowerplus from a nonprofit company in Canada. I thought it was interesting that the company was named, "Truehope." She claimed the micronutrient was supposed to be three times more effective than medication for treating bipolar.

Well, that's not saying much, I thought to myself. Medication had never really benefited me. *Three times zero is still zero.*

I also found myself wary of her claims. Even though medication clearly wasn't helping, I had been told by doctors for years that bipolar was a disorder that could only be treated using medications. How could some vitamins make a difference?

In the end, I decided that I had nothing to lose and was still filled with that indomitable goal to manage my symptoms in any way possible for my family's sake. I had just started putting together my Mood Cycle Survival Guide, and I was open to anything that might mitigate symptoms. I studied Dr. Davies' ruddy face while he studied the documentation I had brought him on the treatment. I was looking for any clue, any validation of the information before him.

As he read, Dr. Davies was occasionally overcome with terrible coughing fits. He'd succumbed to pneumonia the prior winter and never fully recovered.

It concerned me because I'd grown to care for him. He was definitely the first psychiatrist who truly cared for me. Finally, he met my eyes.

"This appears to be a viable option, Michelle." He paused and flipped to the last page of a study. "It's definitely worth a try."

I didn't realize that I had been holding my breath while he was reading. I exhaled. "So, can I just stop taking my medications and start taking the supplements instead?" I questioned.

"Absolutely not!" he responded emphatically. "That would be disastrous."

"What do I do then?" I asked, my eyes wide.

Dr. Davies looked back at the information I had given him and responded, "You will need to get guidance from this company; I'm not familiar with the cross-titration process, but apparently they are." I later learned that cross-titration meant beginning micronutrients and as the brain shows signs of healing *very gradually* and *incrementally* decreasing the dosage of psychotropic medications.

Another coughing fit racked his body and he took a drink from a water bottle on his desk. When he recovered, he looked at me intently and said, "I'll be honest, Michelle, if you had brought this information to me last year I wouldn't have even looked at it."

"Why not?" I asked, caught off guard.

"I've been practicing psychiatry for decades and in medical school we were taught that the only viable treatment for bipolar was pharmaceuticals," he confessed. "And, all of the continuing education is focused on the latest innovations in *medication*." He sighed resignedly. "But nothing else seems to be working for you, so let's give this a try."

At home later that afternoon, I contacted Truehope's customer support and ordered the micronutrients. They set up a file on me in their system. They explained that their goal was to help me navigate the transition from medication to micronutrients as safely and smoothly as possible. I didn't dare trust, but I was willing to try.

After a few weeks of taking EMPowerplus, I started to experience weird, uncomfortable symptoms, the strangest of which was that I could taste the medication in my mouth throughout the day. *Whoa.*

When I asked Dr. Davies about it, he didn't know what to do and suggested

I contact Truehope's customer support again. They told me I was over-medicated and needed to slowly begin reducing my dosages, which I did.

That's when I began to experience fatigue, dizziness, and depression—which I learned were withdrawal symptoms. Even though I felt horrible, I had already been living like that for years! I was resolved to see this through, to finish the process, and discover if the treatment would help. Cross-titration went on for several months, with little improvement.

Just when I thought my condition would never improve, I woke up one morning to something remarkable: My mind was fully *awake*. As I sat up, I let this knowledge cascade over me and I realized I hadn't felt that way in over ten years!

I checked in: I wasn't experiencing mania or the artificial alertness supplied by medication—this was just a sensation of being naturally awake. The fog was gone and there was so much clarity of thought, I sat there marveling.

I called my husband at work and exclaimed, "I think I'm healed!"

"What do you mean?" Scott replied apprehensively.

Why does he sound worried? I wondered. "I feel like my brain is awake for the first time in a decade!" I declared even more emphatically. "I'm not kidding!"

"That's great, sweetie, but maybe you should call your doctor," he insisted, tension clear in his words.

"Scott, I feel fine! I promise I'm not manic; I feel normal! I . . . I just didn't know I could feel like this anymore." I tried to reassure him, "Please don't be worried. I'm just relieved!"

"I'm really happy for you, Michelle," he replied, though I could still hear hints of skepticism.

I couldn't blame Scott for feeling that way after all we'd been through. Even better, his reaction didn't dampen my mood at all. I smiled a wide, authentic smile.

Although I felt a marked improvement that day, my brain was just beginning its healing process. Day after day, month after month over the next year, I began experiencing longer periods of emotional stability and much greater mental clarity. One of the biggest improvements was my sleep. I rarely experienced insomnia any longer. Getting solid, healthy, natural sleep in itself made me a better mom to my children. I was happy to experience being awake and present during the day with my kids, and was much more patient.

During that year, we made a move to Mississippi when Scott was transferred by his company. Liam, now a high-school student, chose to stay in Iowa with his mom and his friends.

Just like any other human being, the process of moving was extremely stressful as I'd found in the past. For me, it triggered symptoms of hypomania—rapid thoughts and sleeping less. Even after the move was complete, I experienced depressive symptoms, but *this* time, things were different. I was able to use my Mood Cycle Survival Guide (MCSG) to manage my symptoms proactively.

This meant I continued meeting the needs of myself and my children—and I recovered much more quickly than I had in the past. As I began to trust my mind more, I started to feel like I could tackle big projects again, armed with my MCSG and my micronutrients. The thought was inspiring to me, and it helped to have Scott's recognition of my recent triumphs too.

Around that year-mark of taking EMPowerplus, I started contemplating something I had wanted to do for years but never believed possible—homeschooling my children. One of my sisters and several friends had homeschooled their children, but in the past, it had felt out of the question for me.

One afternoon, I mentioned my desire to homeschool to my sister—the one who had helped me during my first hospitalization. She was quick to tell me it was a terrible idea and suggested that I might be getting manic. Her words unsettled me. *Am I becoming manic?* Unable to shake my concern, I called Scott at work and told him about the conversation with my sister. By this time in our relationship, we were able to be completely honest with one another regarding my symptoms.

"No, you're not manic, Michelle," he reassured me. "Your sister hasn't seen you since you started this new treatment. This is the most stable you've been since we got married." I was so relieved by his trust and support.

A couple of months later, I took the plunge and began homeschooling my children. It was such a wonderful experience and I was overjoyed to finally be the mother I had always hoped I could be to my children, present and involved on every level.

One of our favorite things to do was go on field trips. Once when we were living in Columbus, Ohio, we went to the zoo. Six-year-old Marcus had just gotten a fun "faux-hawk" haircut and he looked so darling, with his hair sticking up in the middle!

We were having a delightful time, enjoying all the exotic animals. We discovered a bird enclosure where the kids could feed parakeets. One landed on Marcus's matching faux-hawk and he giggled delightedly, lifting the little plastic cup with bird feed to the parakeet. My heart felt like it might explode with joy, accompanied with gratitude that I was well enough to be fully present in that moment with my little boy. Fortunately, those moments were no longer few and far between—they were happening all the time now.

Unexpectedly, nine months later, Scott's job required another move. I was more successful in proactively managing the symptoms this time. I settled into new routines and rhythms quickly that were more manageable with the tools I happily had at my disposal.

I began to notice that my symptoms themselves actually felt different now. They had become significantly less frequent, less intense, and shorter in duration. Feeling much more confident in my mental health, Scott and I made the decision to have one more baby.

Both of us were very aware of the warning from the endocrinologist—that having another baby would destroy my thyroid. Something inside me told me that wouldn't happen, but I still worried that the doctor might be right.

In late May of 2013, while preparing to drive back to Iowa for Liam's high school graduation, I discovered that I was pregnant. *Here we go*, I thought with both hope and apprehension as I stood in the bathroom, staring at the positive pregnancy test.

Quickly, I discovered this pregnancy was significantly different from the first two because I didn't experience the dramatic mood swings. What a relief! The hopeful anticipation of the entire family brought us all together and I had a sweet experience with Gabby and Marcus while at the doctor's when they got to see their little sister on the sonogram monitor. I looked at the awe on the faces of my children and felt tremendous gratitude that I had chosen to stay, chosen to fight, chosen to live.

Josie entered the world pink-faced and perfect on a cold, January afternoon. She was the easiest baby, so happy and smiling. I felt tremendous joy spending my days with my three youngest children. Gabby and Marcus were thrilled with the birth of their little sister and delighted in helping care for her.

Three months came and went and, even as I braced myself for the worst, no postpartum depression symptoms arose! During the entire first year of Josie's life, I watched carefully for any signs of the postpartum hyperthyroidism—but none materialized. I was able to breastfeed her for an entire year until she weaned herself. It felt like a miracle.

Due to this, I began to question what I had been told about my bipolar disorder in the first place. It now seemed a ludicrous suggestion that it could only be treated with drugs. Then I discovered the book, *Anatomy of an Epidemic* by Robert Whitaker.

Whitaker was a science reporter and medical journalist, often writing articles on newly released pharmaceutical drugs. Over time, a question developed in his mind:

If psychiatry had made the great advances in treatment of mental illness that it claimed, why had the number of people permanently disabled by psychiatric disorders *skyrocketed* in the past fifty years? And why were they not getting well?

Whitaker's research conclusions made me feel so outraged, that at first, I had a difficult time finishing the book. I wanted to throw it against the wall, remembering my hospitalizations, my shock therapy, my losing my mind!

That rage, I recognized, came from feeling betrayed by the doctors I had trusted to help me. It was like being robbed of years of my life because I was told I had a mental disease that required medication—and the medication had *harmed* me instead of helping me.

Once I worked through my anger, the knowledge I gained from Whitaker's research was liberating. **I realized it was actually possible to *heal* bipolar disorder. It wasn't a life sentence!**

The Medication Trap

In the beginning of his book, Whitaker shares the history of psychiatry and the origin of psychiatric medications. In the early 1900s, "magic bullet" treatments like penicillin had been discovered that were eradicating formerly deadly diseases. Psychiatry wanted to be part of that medical revolution, but unfortunately, they couldn't identify the underlying causes of the symptoms.

So instead, they created diagnostic categories based on symptoms and then started treating the symptoms with psychotropic medications they had essentially stumbled upon. They didn't think about long-term effects.

> *"By 1970 two possible histories were unfolding. One possibility is that psychiatry, ...stumbled on several types of drugs that, although they produced abnormal behaviors in animals, nevertheless fixed various abnormalities in the brain chemistry of those who were mentally ill... The other possibility is that psychiatry, eager to have its own magic pills and eager to take its place in mainstream medicine, turned the drugs into something they were not."* (Whitaker, Robert. *Anatomy of an Epidemic.*)

Psychiatry then tried to come up with a way to justify the use of medications to treat symptoms without a known pathology. That gave rise to the chemical imbalance theory. When I was first diagnosed in 1998 with bipolar, I was told that I had a chemical imbalance and medication would balance my brain chemistry. I didn't know it at the time, but that theory had already been debunked! "Mental disorders have also been touted to the public as diseases caused by chemical imbalances, but there was never any evidence to support those claims." (Whitaker, Robert. *Anatomy of an Epidemic.)*

Likewise, the story I was told about bipolar being the same as having diabetes and the medication like insulin was just that: a story. There was no scientific basis for the claim, but it continued to be used to lend too much credibility to the idea that bipolar was a clearly delineated medical problem with a defined, effective course of treatment. The comparison was false.

Over time, when people presented with symptoms that didn't fit into those created medical categories, psychiatry expanded the parameters of the diagnosis. Psychotropic medications were then used to treat the symptoms without consideration for the long-term efficacy or impact of the drugs on the mind and body.

The result?

"Researchers determined that the drugs work by perturbing the normal functioning of neuronal pathways in the brain. In response, the brain undergoes "compensatory adaptations" to cope with the drug's mucking up of its messaging system, and this leaves the brain functioning in an "abnormal" manner. Rather than fix chemical imbalances in the brain, the drugs create them." (Whitaker, Robert. *Anatomy of an Epidemic.*)

Even worse, not only are psychotropic drugs not addressing the cause of the bipolar symptoms, but the long-term impact on the body and brain does additional, sometimes permanent damage.

"This is also a form of care that leads to early death. The seriously mentally ill are now dying fifteen to twenty-five years earlier than normal, with this problem of early death having become much more pronounced in the past fifteen years. They are dying from cardiovascular ailments, respiratory problems, metabolic illnesses, diabetes, kidney failure, and so forth—the physical ailments tend to pile up as people stay on antipsychotics (or drug cocktails) for years on end." (Whitaker, Robert. *Anatomy of an Epidemic.*)

Although some people may get a bit of short-term relief from symptoms with the use of psychotropic medications, the reality is that they are not treating the source of their "disorder." According to the National Institute for Mental Health's own website to this day, it states, "the exact cause of bipolar disorder is unknown."[1]

I believe that ultimately the reason that bipolar disorder has become a chronic, progressive, incurable mental illness is the paradigm of *treatment*

---

[1] www.nimh.nih.gov/health/publications/bipolar-disorder.

with psychiatric medications. It is not that bipolar cannot be healed; it is that the pharmaceutical approach to treatment *prevents* healing.

Once I read Robert Whitaker's book, the answer to all the confusion, frustration, and pain of the twelve years I had been taking psychotropic drugs became crystal clear. I did not need medication like insulin. My disorder wasn't chronic and incurable! I could, in fact, heal. I was already healing—I just had to give my brain what it needed to function in a healthy, balanced way.

Getting off of medication and finding EMPowerplus cleared the way for me to begin healing the other underlying causes of my symptoms, which I will discuss in the following chapters. I was so grateful that my friend Peggy had had enough courage to introduce specialized high-quality micronutrients to me, and now I had healed to the point I wanted to shout it from the rooftops to anyone else who was suffering the way I had.

WARNING: If you decide to switch from medication to micronutrients, DO NOT go off of medication "cold turkey," or stop all at once. Medication alters your brain chemistry and withdrawal symptoms can be dangerous, even life-threatening. DO work closely with someone specifically trained in cross-titration–either Truehope customer support or a trusted psychiatrist who has been specifically trained in cross-titration–to safely withdraw from the drugs and transition to the micronutrients that will help heal your brain.

Healing the Brain with ... Vitamins?

If you're like me when you are first presented with the idea of using micronutrients to treat bipolar, you might be incredulous. "How can vitamins help my bipolar?" you might wonder, and you are not alone. In the book, *The Better Brain*, by Bonnie Kaplan, PhD and Julia Rucklidge, PhD, they come straight out and share that:

"Many people find it hard to believe that 'just' nutrition could solve mental health problems. This attitude isn't just wrong. It's wrong,

outdated, and harmful — especially because there have been dozens and dozens of rigorous scientific studies showing that nutrition can be a vital key for preventing and treating mental disorders." (Kaplan, Bonnie and Julia Rucklidge. *The Better Brain.*)

What are micronutrients?

You may likely be familiar with the macronutrients our bodies need: protein, fat, and carbohydrates. "Macro," meaning large, refers to larger molecules and we need these in larger quantities because they provide the fuel for our bodies. "Micro" on the other hand, means small, because these molecules are smaller and we need smaller quantities of these particular nutrients. Simply put, micronutrients are vitamins and minerals that the body needs to function in a healthy way.

Even though we need micronutrients in smaller quantities, they are nevertheless critical to our brains.

> *"Our brains demand a disproportionately large amount of the nutrients we consume. . .Most Americans don't know that the brain metabolism responsible for the production of neurotransmitters like serotonin and dopamine is dependent on an ample supply of micronutrients. . .We now know that there are many people with underlying risk factors, often genetic, that may make them more vulnerable to emotional distress when their diet is poor. Improve and fix their nutritional needs, and many of them can and will get better."* (Kaplan, Bonnie and Julia Rucklidge. *The Better Brain.*)

A Story of Truehope

I was feeling so good that I wanted to do some research to understand my results more fully. I learned that EMPowerplus was developed in the 1990s in direct response to two people suffering from bipolar. One of the founders of the company, Anthony Stephan, had lost his wife and father-in-law both to suicide after they had suffered with bipolar for years. Two of Anthony's children, Joseph, a teenager, and Autumn, a young married mother of one, were also suffering horribly with the disorder and psychotropic drugs were not helping.

Anthony had exhausted all medical avenues to help his children. Autumn was in and out of psychiatric facilities, unable to care for herself or her baby. One of the top pediatric psychiatrists in the country said there was nothing more that could be done for Joseph and he would likely be institutionalized.

Desperate to save his children's lives, Anthony turned to a friend, David Hardy, who had worked in the field of farm animal nutrition for many years. David wondered if micronutrient deficiencies, which caused irritability and aggression in farm animals might play a role in human bipolar symptoms. Together, Tony and David formulated a nutritional supplement program that they administered first to Joseph and later to Autumn.

Ultimately both Joseph and Autumn were able to use micronutrients to eliminate psychotropic medications and completely recover from their symptoms.[2] The two men formed Truehope and spent the following two decades refining their product specifically for brain health. Eventually, the company partners split up: Anthony Stephan kept Truehope and David Hardy formed Hardy Nutritionals.

I saw the hopelessness of my own ordeal mirrored in the experiences of Joseph and Autumn. As I read about Anthony's determination and perseverance, I felt overwhelming gratitude. The treatment he developed for his children had changed my life and granted me the same freedom from psychotropic drugs, clearing the way for me to heal.

During that same time, a growing number of doctors and scientists around the world were beginning to research the role of nutrition in treating mental illness. As knowledge of EMPowerplus began to spread, researchers decided to run independent studies on the treatment, with Dr. Kaplan conducting some of the earliest studies, published beginning in 2001. The results were astonishing.

To date, more than fifty peer-reviewed studies of these multi-nutrient formulas have been published by scientists who are independent of the

---

[2] www.truehope.com/about/the-truehope-story.

companies.[34] These were the studies that convinced Dr. Davies that this treatment was a viable alternative to medication for me. I will forever be grateful to my doctor for being open-minded enough to look at the information and frankly, caring more about my welfare than his ego. I also think it's important to emphasize that the doctors and scientists in these trials didn't receive a dime from Truehope or Hardy Nutritionals.

I need to bring up that there is a reason in this book that I focus on EMPowerplus. It's because it is the supplement that has been so helpful for me, and I did try two alternative multivitamin supplements from other companies, each claiming their product was the best on the market and highly absorbable. In the beginning, I compared the ingredient labels to the ingredients in EMPowerplus, and they seemed similar so I thought they would work the same. Yet, each time within a couple of weeks of switching, I felt myself becoming symptomatic. In both cases after only two months, I switched back to EMPowerplus.

In their book, *The Better Brain*, Kaplan and Rucklidge warn that when using a micronutrient treatment to treat mental illness, it is important to seek out a treatment that has been independently verified and proven effective.

"99 percent of OTC supplements have never been tested at all for health benefits! Even fewer have been evaluated by independent scientists — people not biased by any affiliation with the manufacturer. Does that mean these supplements won't help? We don't know. If they contain a similar breadth of ingredients to those studied at similar doses, then maybe they will. We can't recommend them if there is no published science behind them." (Kaplan, Bonnie and Julia Rucklidge. *The Better Brain*.)

I have grown to trust EMPowerplus not only because of the effect it had on me personally, but also because of the science behind it. I have never and will never receive any compensation for advocating for Truehope's

---

[3] www.truehope.com/research.

[4] www.hardynutritionals.com/studies.

micronutrient treatment—just like the scientists who have studied it. I believe in EMPowerplus and want anyone else who is suffering the way I did to know about it so that they can begin their own path to healing.

When I share what I've learned about micronutrients, people often talk about having blood tests that show they aren't deficient in any nutrients. In their book, Drs. Kaplan and Rucklidge explain, *"Blood tests are not necessary for deciding on treatment, nor are they generally helpful. . .what is being tested is the circulating level of the nutrient in your body, not your brain. And no test can determine what your brain actually needs."* (Kaplan, Bonnie and Julia Rucklidge. *The Better Brain.*)

I learned over the years that the best indicator of a nutrient deficiency is actually the symptoms. I worked closely with Truehope to identify what nutrients my brain needed in order to heal and function in a healthy, balanced way. Self-awareness and communication were key to success.

Cross-titration: What I Wish I'd Known

Looking back, I am grateful that I never gave up, especially when I faced challenges while my brain was healing. Years of being conditioned to believe I needed medication made me feel nervous when I would experience any old, familiar symptoms. Since then, I learned some valuable lessons that I will share with you now. These tips will help cross-titration go more smoothly and the understanding of what to expect will make it easier to trust the process.

Work with an Expert

First, it is critical that you work closely with someone knowledgeable and experienced in cross-titration. Truehope has developed a thorough, effective cross-titration protocol. They are aware that it is very difficult to find doctors open to micronutrient treatment and even more rare to find one trained in cross-titration. To bridge that gap, they created a thoroughly trained customer support department to provide guidance and answers as you go through the process.

There are challenges created by withdrawal and overmedication symptoms. It can also take time to pinpoint your unique nutritional needs. Truehope has been refining their knowledge over the past two decades and will help you be successful. I know I wouldn't be as healed as I am today without their assistance.

When working with cross-titration experts, keep these tips in mind:

- Make sure you **provide complete and accurate information**. There are a number of variables that can impact the cross-titration process. I didn't realize for years that a different supplement I was taking contained a key ingredient that interfered with the absorption of EMPowerplus. Once I discovered this conflict and discontinued the other supplement, the EMPowerplus became more effective.

  Be open about medications or supplements you currently take or have taken, the length of time, diagnoses you have, and any illicit drug use in your past. Just like your doctors, the more information they have, the better equipped they will be in assisting you toward healing.
- **Track your symptoms and moods** by using the Bearable app (introduced in the previous chapter) or another tracking system. Communicate what you are experiencing consistently with Truehope or your cross-titration expert. This can be as often as two or three times a week in the beginning. When I was first starting cross-titration, I spoke with customer support two to three times a week for the first couple months. It can sometimes be challenging to know what to share because symptoms have often become normal to us, so we don't realize they are indications of a missing nutrient.

  For the first few years after I began taking EMPowerplus, I felt a huge improvement in my major symptoms. One thing I continued to struggle with was anger. I didn't view this as a symptom, however; I thought it was a character flaw. One day I was on the phone with Truehope and I happened to mention the frustration I experienced with agitation and angry outbursts. The support person indicated that I needed to add salmon oil to my daily intake. I followed her advice on dosing, and within a few days the agitation and anger were gone! Years of beating myself up for what I believed was a lack of self-control were resolved because of a missing nutrient.

Symptoms are information and can indicate withdrawal, overmedication, or a need for an adjustment in micronutrients. Prompt communication and accurate information will enable customer support to guide you through the process more smoothly.

Be Consistent

Second, consistency in taking your medications and micronutrients is essential. While you are going through cross-titration and beyond, it will be one of the most important, if not the most important, thing you do each day. I found that I needed to use pill organizers to simplify the process of taking the pills—I organized them each Sunday using an alarm to remind me. I also used alarms throughout the day to remind me to take the pills.

It can be tricky when you are still taking medications because there needs to be time between when you take meds and when you take the micronutrients. Using alarms and keeping the pills with you throughout the day if you are away from home will help you be successful. In addition, labeling and preparing in advance for any travel helps keep your ongoing needs for brain nutrition met.

Be Patient

Third, be patient. Recognize and embrace the fact that it takes time to heal. If you are starting with *no* medication in your body, keep in mind it can take up to three months to feel a difference. Stick with it until you give yourself the chance to feel different, better.

If you are starting with psychotropic medications in your body, it can take longer. *"If you are transitioning from medication to nutrients, psychiatrists' reports indicate you should give it at least six months to a year, as the transition can be challenging."* (Kaplan, Bonnie and Julia Rucklidge. *The Better Brain.*) I promise you, it is worth it.

One key piece that helped me remain patient through this process was keeping in mind my end goal: I knew I couldn't choose to leave this planet without ruining my daughter's life. Along with the realization that I couldn't live as well as I deserved by just "suffering well," I kept my determined mind-set of not giving up. With patience, healing will come, for each of us.

Med-release

Fourth, I learned that medication can actually stay in your soft tissues for years! [5] Stress or intense exercise can push those chemicals back out into your body. This is called a "med-release," and when they get in your bloodstream, they can cause a recurrence of symptoms.

This happened to me four times over the ten years after I started on the micronutrients. The stress of moving my family to another location and even training for triathlons caused these med-releases, each time resulting in depression. I learned quickly to contact Truehope when this happened, and they walked me through the protocol for safely getting the medication out of my system. Within days, I felt better.

> **WARNING: Popular over-the-counter detox cleanses can be extremely harmful for those who have been on psychotropic medications—especially for those on them for years. Cleanses can trigger med-release and severe symptoms.[6]**

Once when a med-release happened, I reasoned that it would be better just to do a cleanse to get all of the medication out at once. Truehope's customer support warned me strongly against this course of action, telling me that there was no way to know how much medication was still in my body and that it could be disastrous. Unfortunately, I didn't listen to them and tried anyway. Going against their warnings caused me to become severely depressed. I regretted it quickly and never went against their advice again.

---

[5] https://www.merckmanuals.com/en-ca/professional/clinical-pharmacology/pharmacokinetics/drug
-distribution-to-tissues.

[6] https://www.merckmanuals.com/en-ca/professional/clinical-pharmacology/pharmacokinetics/drug
-distribution-to-tissues.

Maintain Healthy Digestion

Fifth, keep your gut healthy. If your stomach and intestines are unhealthy and unable to absorb the micronutrients effectively, it won't matter how much of them you take. There are things that can cause your body to get out of balance so that you are unable to absorb nutrients properly, like taking antibiotics. Anytime you take antibiotics or have any other digestive issues, contact Truehope to learn how to restore healthy absorption.

When I finally completed the cross-titration process and my brain began to heal, I was able to utilize other tools of healing effectively in combination. While I had gone to therapy periodically during the time I was on medication and tried to use the coping mechanisms that my therapists suggested, the problem was that traditional medications were getting in the way. They had, in a sense, hijacked my brain and made it difficult (sometimes impossible), to work on healing other aspects of my mind—past trauma, unhealthy coping mechanisms, unhealthy thought and behavior patterns, and more.

Once I gave my brain what it needed to function in a healthy way–safely eliminating psychotropic medications–I was capable of moving forward on the path to healing the other underlying causes of my symptoms.

CHAPTER 7

STEP THREE-THERAPY:
Why Did I Wait So Long?

Three years before I ever dreamed something like micronutrients could heal my brain, I was at wits end, and succumbed to trying another therapist. *I need help!* I thought in desperation as I drove to my counseling appointment one fall afternoon. That morning I had lost control and screamed at fifteen-month-old Marcus. All I could think was, *I want to be a good mom and I don't know how to control this rage!*

As I drove the half hour to the appointment, I reflected on my frustrating history with therapists. This was my third one in five years. My German psychiatrist in Chicago had encouraged therapy to learn coping skills to manage my symptoms, but nothing that practitioner taught me seemed to make a difference. The symptoms I experienced took over and I was just along for the ride.

The next clinician I saw had been completely useless. I'd met with her once a week for four months, and each visit, I would talk for the entire fifty minutes while she took notes. When the appointment was over, she would glance at the clock and say, "Oh, times up! See you next week."

I always left her office thinking, *What a waste of money! I could do that for free with a friend!* and eventually quit going.

Finally, Dr. Davies had convinced me to give therapy another try. I had been seeing this new therapist for a few weeks and was doing my best to stay open-minded. When I arrived in the parking lot, I sat for a minute in my car, trying to collect my thoughts. *I can figure out how to be a good mom*, I thought determinedly, *I just need some support and guidance.*

In my appointment, I poured out my broken heart to my counselor. "When this happens, I feel like I'm having an out-of-body experience," I shared disconsolately. "I lose control and then I feel so ashamed of myself when it's over."

She nodded thoughtfully, taking notes as I described my outburst. When I finished speaking, she looked at me for a minute and then finally replied, "Michelle, some women just aren't cut out to be mothers. I recommend that you put your children in daycare and go back to work."

I sat there in stunned silence for several minutes. Then something inside me rose up in rebellion. *No! That is not the answer! God did not set me up to fail. There has to be a way to fix this!*

I left her office that day, never to see her again.

During my hospitalizations, I was assigned therapists who helped me create safety plans and identify stressors in my life, but it didn't seem to go beyond that. I began to view therapy as a sort of triage to get through emergencies.

As I continued to develop and utilize the Mood Cycle Survival Guide (MCSG), I became more self-aware through my Early Warning System. I recognized symptoms that were being triggered by situations or people; however, I wasn't sure what to do about that, other than to avoid the stressors or prepare for the inevitable, emotional upheaval.

Then, six years after my last therapy "session," we experienced a significant stressor when Scott lost his job and struggled to find a new one for almost two years. The prolonged, intense strain was more than I could handle and I became persistently depressed. Our church minister encouraged me to seek counseling. Feeling like it couldn't hurt, I agreed to give therapy one more try.

In my first session with Heather, I confessed to her my negative experiences with past practitioners. "I want to be proactive at finding ways to cope with stress so I don't end up anxious and depressed," I said. "I don't want to just talk about my problems, I want to solve them."

Heather responded with understanding and reassurance that our sessions would not only be interactive but very proactive. During that first visit, we set goals for our work together—my first time ever having a clinician do that with me! I began to hope that perhaps this would indeed be different.

Over the next several months, Heather kept her promise. She introduced me to "therapy modalities," specialized approaches that could be utilized to address different concerns. She utilized art to help uncover issues I was struggling with but couldn't verbalize easily, games that were used in a session Gabby attended to help open up communication and connection, and EMDR (Eye Movement Desensitization and Reprocessing) for trauma healing.

My first experience with EMDR really piqued my interest. I had been struggling with some intense emotions for a couple weeks so she asked me to think back to the earliest memory I had where I remembered feeling those same emotions to that intensity. I immediately recalled an experience in my childhood and shared that with her. She nodded, then invited me to sit facing her with my eyes closed while she tapped my knees alternately with her hands. As she tapped, she invited me to talk about the experience and what I felt.

Occasionally when the emotions would get really intense in terms of tears, she paused and invited me to sit back and take a deep breath. When I calmed, we would resume. This went on for about half an hour until I was all cried out.

When we were finished, Heather asked me to consider the same memory again—and I was surprised to recognize that my feelings about it had *changed*. No longer did I experience the raw, painful emotions but felt almost detached from them. Suddenly, that sad and painful childhood memory didn't evoke an intense emotional response anymore. I was shocked—and pleased. For me, that success was something that had never happened before, let alone while in therapy.

That evening when I returned home, Scott noticed that I seemed unusually calm. "Hey, are you okay? How was your appointment?" he asked.

"I don't know how to describe what I just experienced," I responded, still in awe. "It was like having poison sucked out of my body. I want to do it again!"

A short time later, Scott finally found a job and we needed to move to Utah. After this initial success, I hoped I could continue with Heather virtually, but was very disappointed to discover that she was prohibited by law from working with clients out of state. With my track record with therapists, I was reticent about starting over with someone new, but I had finally seen the value in therapy with a *good* therapist.

This time I did my homework before I started. I read up on different treatment modalities, including Cognitive Behavioral Therapy and more about EMDR. I looked up clinics that offered the modalities that I was interested in and interviewed the heads of each clinic. I settled on a practice that had several practitioners who specialized in trauma therapy and EMDR in particular. Then I set up an appointment with a therapist named Shirley.

What Is Therapy?

Working with Shirley was life-changing. I finally began to understand the purpose of therapy: it was a tool, and my therapist was a facilitator who guided me in the use of that tool. Working together, we identified triggers and underlying causes of symptoms. Then, utilizing her education and training, she suggested appropriate modalities to help me process, resolve, or remove those triggers. I felt safe, proactive, and like life was getting better in ways I had never experienced before. That, I came to know, was what *good* therapy looked like.

Unhealthy Boundaries

My initial therapy goals were focused on improving my relationships with Scott and my children. One of the first things we worked on was boundaries. I learned that in order to have healthy relationships with my husband, children, and others, I needed to establish healthy boundaries for myself and learn to respect the boundaries of others.

During one session when we were discussing this topic, I interrupted Shirley and sheepishly admitted, "I don't really understand what boundaries are."

Shirley kindly reassured me that it was a topic that many people didn't understand. She proceeded to teach me, using the analogy of borders on a map. A country has boundary lines around it. Within its borders, the country has the right to decide who and what they will allow into their territory. It also has responsibilities to its citizens for care and protection. To maintain peace, it is essential for countries to respect each other's boundaries. "Healthy boundaries lead to healthy relationships," concluded Shirley with a smile.

This explanation helped me to recognize my responsibilities for myself and changes I needed to make in my interactions with my family and others.

Unhealthy Thought and Behavior Patterns

Unhealthy thought and behavior patterns can trigger symptoms. Identifying thoughts and behaviors as unhealthy was a challenge, though, because they were habitual and felt normal to me.

Another thing that Shirley helped me to recognize was that many of my thought patterns were unhealthy. They had developed based on the false idea that I needed to change to be acceptable, rooted deeply in my childhood bullying. I would compulsively change to suit whatever people or circumstances I was around. These thoughts and behaviors were triggers for symptoms of anxiety and depression.

One of the therapy modalities that was helpful in this area was Cognitive Behavioral Therapy (CBT). According to the book, *Mind Over Mood,* by Dennis Greenberger, PhD and Christine A. Padesky, PhD:

> *"'Cognitive' refers to what we think and how we think...A central idea in CBT is that our thoughts about an event or experience powerfully affects our emotional, behavioral, and physical responses to it."*

The other modality that was beneficial to me was Mindfulness Based Cognitive Therapy (MBCT). This form of therapy was developed using mindfulness meditation, which helped me become aware of my thoughts and how they affected my mental and emotional states. Mindfulness meditation will be explored more thoroughly in Chapter 8.

Unhealthy Coping Mechanisms

In a session with Shirley one day, I was sharing my discouragement over what I deemed my television "addiction," and she asked, "What need is being met when you are watching TV?"

I was taken aback by her question. I had felt for years that my compulsion to watch endless hours of TV while neglecting my family and my own self-care was a moral flaw. As we discussed the behavior and the circumstances that surrounded my "binge-watching," I learned that it was a coping mechanism signaling an underlying distress.

Shirley taught me that coping mechanisms are a natural response to stress or distress. Some people develop coping mechanisms like overeating, compulsive spending, and even addictions to drugs or self-harm that point to an underlying wound or mental distress that needs to be processed and healed. I learned to start paying attention (using my MCSG), to events or circumstances that seemed to trigger the urge to watch television and started working with Shirley to address the underlying issues.

Unhealed Trauma

The first two years that I worked with Shirley were hard, consistent, necessary work that I faced head on. We continued peeling back layers of unhealthy thought and behavior patterns, boundaries, and coping mechanisms I had developed over my lifetime.

Shirley was a perfect fit for me. She was well-read and recognized my interest in self-help books, occasionally recommending some that would allow me to dive deeper into certain topics.

As my trust in her grew, I became more open with her. Still, I carefully avoided anything to do with my previous marriage, except to mention it in passing as part of my history. *It's in the past*, I reasoned to myself. *I've moved on and I don't need to talk about it.* In all my years working with various therapists, I had NEVER wanted to talk about it. As I eventually began working with micronutrients to heal my mind and get so much better, however, *that* unhealed wound became more pronounced.

My trust in therapy and my desire to improve my relationship with Scott led us to seek marriage counseling. One day in a session, it became apparent that the unaddressed trauma from my marriage to Alex was greatly impacting my marriage to Scott. *How can that be?* I thought in shock. *That was over twenty-five years ago!*

As the truth of the realization sunk in, however, and memory after memory of hurt, betrayal, and pain came to the forefront, I became determined to face all of it. It was time to do the work to heal, especially the parts that I'd been shying away from for so long.

My fingers trembled as I wrote the email to my therapist:

Shirley, I need to do EMDR to process the trauma from my first marriage to Alex.

My chest tightened and my eyes brimmed with tears. I paused to take a breath and pray for support. *Please, Heavenly Father, help me have the courage and strength to face this*, I entreated.

Shirley responded by getting me in within a few days. I had done EMDR only for smaller traumas in the past and thought I knew what to expect, but I wasn't prepared for the Pandora's box I was opening.

During the first half of the session, I shared memories I had from my marriage to Alex. There was one instance in particular that stood out for me and Shirley suggested we work on processing that experience.

I took a steadying breath as she handed me the pulsers—two plastic paddles that I could hold in the palms of my hands. They were attached by wires to a control box and they would vibrate back and forth as I held them. I had learned previously from Shirley that there were different approaches to EMDR, and this was her preferred method.

Sitting up in my seat and gripping the pulsers, I closed my eyes and Shirley prompted me with a question about the memory. Twenty minutes later, the session was over. There was a pile of tissue next to me on the couch and I felt like I'd run a marathon.

"We have opened up a lot of trauma in this session," Shirley said gently as I sagged exhausted on the couch. "Your mind is going to continue processing this. Which of your self-care tools will you use to manage that?"

"I'm so tired right now," I said dully. "I think I just want to watch a movie when I get home."

"I think that's a good idea," she replied with a smile. "Our next appointment is in a week. Email me if you need any help before then."

That evening I discovered what she meant. My body suddenly felt like I was back in my marriage to Alex—my chest was gripped in a vice, my heart racing with intense fear and panic. I was overwhelmed by feelings of worthlessness and shame. It was disorienting because I could *see* that I was safe, in my home with Scott and my children, but my entire being was consumed by the very real feelings of the terrified, emotionally damaged nineteen-year-old.

Scott wanted to help but he didn't understand what I was experiencing and didn't know what to do. I was so confused, too, that I wasn't even sure what to ask for. I spent the entire night sobbing, curled up in the fetal position on the floor of an empty room in our house.

I reached out to Shirley and she got me in quickly. From there we worked together twice a week. She helped me understand better what was happening between sessions. Unprocessed trauma, I rapidly discovered, was like having a broken leg that healed wrong so it constantly caused pain and other problems within the body. EMDR was like rebreaking the bone, resetting it, and allowing it to heal properly.

It quickly became apparent that I also needed to eliminate any unnecessary stressors in my life. I was undertaking an emotional healing process that made me extremely vulnerable and raw. Just as Shirley suggested, I focused on important self-care tools—mindfulness meditation, grounding yoga, and simple exercise.

Scott, ever my partner and #1 supporter, helped lighten my load of household responsibilities to give me time to rest more; I needed a lot of sleep—and needed to not feel guilty about it.

After a month and a half, there was one day when I woke up filled with nearly overwhelming rage. I was shocked by the intensity of the feelings but recognized that it was different from the explosive, triggered outbursts I'd experienced when my children were little. I was able to maintain self-control and steered clear of my family most of the day in order to avoid saying something horrible to anyone like I regrettably had in the past. I went to bed early that night because I just needed the day to end.

When I woke up the next morning, my mind and body were peacefully calm. I wasn't sure if I could trust the feeling to last after so many weeks of turmoil, but I decided to be grateful, even if it was a temporary reprieve.

Later in the day as I drove to my scheduled session with my therapist, I tentatively allowed myself to think about the memories I had been processing. I wanted to prepare myself for the return of the intense emotions, but oddly I didn't feel anything.

When I walked into Shirley's office, I told her about the "day of rage."

"Oh!" she exclaimed with a grin. "I'm so glad!"

Startled, I asked, "Why?"

"Because anger is usually the last phase of the healing process!" she responded with enthusiasm.

That session was completely different. As we discussed each of the triggering memories, she asked, "How do you feel about that?"

"If I were there again, I would tell him 'NO!' and I would leave!" I declared with an intensity that stunned me. I felt no emotional attachment to the memories anymore. Instead, I was filled with fresh feelings of confidence and clarity that what had happened to me was wrong—that I didn't deserve it and never had.

As I drove home, I felt an extraordinary sense of lightness and relief. *Why had I waited so long to process those memories?* I wondered to myself.

One of the most surprising results of the EMDR therapy was discovering how many triggers and unhealthy thoughts and behaviors had been rooted in the trauma caused by my first marriage. Here's the important part: many of them were simply *gone* now because the reason they developed in the first place was faced and resolved.

What Just Happened?

My ever-curious brain was captivated by what I had experienced, so I began reading books about healing and trauma therapy. The most profound insights came from, *The Body Keeps the Score,* by Bessel van der Kolk, M.D. In his book, he goes in-depth into the psychological, emotional, mental, and physiological impact of trauma. He shares different healing modalities that can address the resulting dysregulation.

Dr. Van der Kolk warned about the problems produced by creating medical diagnoses based on symptoms, then treating them with psychotropic drugs.

"How do we treat people who are coping with the fall-out of abuse, betrayal and abandonment when we are forced to diagnose them with depression, panic disorder, bipolar illness, or borderline personality, which do not really address what they are coping with?" (Van der Kolk, Bessel. *The Body Keeps the Score.*)

In his book, Van der Kolk validated some truths that I was just beginning to realize in my own life. He advocates for identifying and treating the *causes* of symptoms using appropriate modalities to help the person heal.

> *"'Many psychiatrists today work in assembly-line offices where they see patients they hardly know for fifteen minutes and then dole out pills to relieve pain, anxiety or depression. . .Be compliant and take these drugs and come back in three months—but be sure not to use alcohol or (illegal) drugs to relieve your problems.' Such shortcuts in treatment make it impossible to develop self-care and self-leadership. . .Our increasing use of drugs to treat these conditions doesn't address the real issues."* (Van der Kolk, Bessel. *The Body Keeps the Score*.)

When I first went to a psychiatrist for evaluation, the doctor based his diagnosis on the symptoms I described. How might my experience have been different if there was exploration into my personal history and acknowledgement that the symptoms were, at least in part, a natural reaction of my body and brain coping with trauma?

The main reason I resisted therapy for so many years was a fundamental misunderstanding of the purpose of therapy, and how to use it effectively to heal. I wish someone had just taken the time to teach me the basics about how therapy—not drugs—could be proactively used toward my healing. That would have dispelled so many of my misconceptions and made a huge difference in how much I suffered in the meantime.

How to Use Therapy Proactively

Between utilizing my MCSG and working with Heather and Shirley, I have learned how to use therapy proactively and effectively. These are the top tips I discovered to help you be successful in utilizing this tool in your own healing journey.

Finding the RIGHT Therapist

Not all therapists are competent and they won't all be a good fit for you. It is essential to have someone that you trust and feel comfortable opening up to, so that therapy will be effective. If you start seeing a practitioner and you don't feel it is a suitable match, own your voice and take a stand for your mental health. Part ways and find a new one. **This tool will only be effective if you are comfortable in the relationship with your clinician.**

It is also important to find someone to work with that will help you be proactive. You should set goals for your work together, and over time, discuss different modalities that could be effective in helping you work toward those goals. Your therapist should shift and grow with you, and always be working diligently with you as you heal.

It will be important to explore different therapeutic modalities to find what will be most effective for your specific needs. Some that I have experienced personally are art, play, attachment, EMDR, mindfulness based cognitive therapy (MBCT), cognitive behavioral therapy (CBT), and Emotional Freedom Technique (EFT or tapping).

IMPORTANT NOTE: Although it worked well for me, EMDR is not the only trauma therapy or always the most effective trauma therapy available. Different types of trauma and different traumatic experiences may necessitate alternative therapy approaches. Some additional trauma therapies to consider are Rapid Resolution Therapy, Internal Family Systems, and Somatic Therapy. (This list is not exhaustive). If you have a history of severe dissociation or severe childhood trauma, EMDR may not be advisable. Consult with your specialist for personalized and effective care.

Each clinician will specialize or be trained in specific modalities. As you progress in your healing journey, your needs may evolve, requiring a different approach and potentially a change in practitioners. Stay open-minded and do your research to make sure you're always working with people who are certified in the skill sets that serve you best. Remember: therapy is a tool and the therapist is a facilitator. You need to find a competent facilitator.

Give Your Therapist Something to Work With

Therapists are not mind readers or magicians. The only information they have to work with is what you share with them. Sometimes this can be difficult because you don't always know what to talk about. Over time, I discovered that paying attention to experiences and circumstances that triggered symptoms was a good place to start. Your MCSG, journaling, and mood-tracking apps are excellent resources that can help you become more self-aware.

It is also important not to withhold information from your practitioner. This goes back to making sure you have a clinician you can trust. A good therapist is able to hold the information you provide without judgment. It can take time to develop a deep enough comfort level to share, especially personal or traumatic experiences, but if you continually find yourself holding back, it might be wise to ask yourself why.

The focus of the therapist is to help you work through uncomfortable and painful experiences in order to come to a place of mental wellness and healing. The more complete the picture you provide, the better he or she will be able to help you.

Be Proactive, Not Just Reactive

If you are only seeking therapy as a source of emotional triage when you are in crisis, like I did in the beginning, it can be counterproductive for many reasons. First, the process of establishing yourself with a new therapist can be exhausting and sometimes intimidating. If you wait until you are in an emergency to seek help, the emotional effort required can become a barrier.

It can also give a skewed picture to the clinician if they only observe you in *turmoil*. The longer you see a professional and the more varied the emotional states they witness, the better they will understand you and your needs.

I finally realized that by being proactive I could utilize therapy to heal the triggers and eventually prevent the crisis from occurring in the first place.

Focus on Healing, Not Blaming

Something that I have found to be a challenge in therapy is that it is easy to get focused on a person or persons who have caused you harm. You have no control over what someone else says or does, and it can turn you into a victim who continues to be traumatized. This is disempowering.

Instead, think about emotional or mental injury the way you would a physical injury. If you broke your leg, you would go to the hospital for help. To help the doctor properly assess the injury, you would describe how it happened, but then the focus would be on healing, not the person who caused the harm. It would also be important to establish healthy boundaries to protect against a repeat injury.

This approach is empowering and will aid recovery much more than if you spend all of your time focused on the person who hurt you. You can't control their choices, but you can choose to both heal and protect yourself.

IMPORTANT NOTE: From my experiences, I recognize that there may be relationships in your life where your healthy boundaries won't work because the other person is unhealthy and can continue to hurt you mentally, physically, emotionally, sexually, spiritually, or in other ways. Work with a great therapist and assess the situation. If it is dangerous, get out. Then continue to do the work that needs to be done to heal. Only accept relationships where your healthy boundaries—and theirs—are respected.

You Get Out What You Put In

You need to actively participate not just in sessions with your therapist but in doing the "homework" between sessions. Sometimes we want things to be simple and easy—"take a pill and you'll feel better." But the reality is that therapy is not easy. It takes effort, bravery, and commitment to discover your unhealthy thoughts and behaviors, unhealed trauma, and unhealthy boundaries. Then you have to work to process them and especially to replace them with healthy alternatives.

If you are not willing to put in the effort during sessions, and (more importantly), between sessions, therapy will not be productive or helpful. You and your therapist can identify priorities to focus on between sessions in your day-to-day life that will help you make vital shifts in your thinking and interactions. You can set reminders to help you follow through on what you committed to do. This will help you experience real change and progress in improving your mental health.

Therapy Takes Time

Therapy is like peeling back layers of an onion. When you begin this process, there may be pressing concerns that at first feel like they are the only difficulties. As you set goals and work on them, you will likely uncover other issues that need your attention. Keep going. This is where the deeper healing begins.

When I decided to be proactive about therapy, I jokingly said, "I'm going to go until I have nothing left to talk about!" After working with Shirley for about two years, I was getting to that point where I felt like I was done. But I decided to continue seeing her on a "maintenance" basis for another year—with Shirley that was once a month. It turned out to be a wise decision. During that third year was when I realized I needed to process the trauma from my first marriage. Without acknowledging that need for time to pass, I wouldn't have discovered that huge turning point.

Therapy takes time and patience. If you follow the tips I've shared here, it will lead you further down the path to healing. In the next chapter, we will discuss mindfulness meditation. This tool will not only be a hugely beneficial self-care tool but will also enable you to become more self-aware and productive in therapy.

CHAPTER 8

STEP FOUR-MINDFULNESS MEDITATION:
Becoming Friends with My Mind

I felt my chest tightening and my body going rigid. I recognized the signs of being triggered, and although I kept telling myself, *this is an irrational reaction, stop it!* my body ignored my pleas to calm down.

It was early morning in late July and our family was getting ready to spend the day with Scott's company for their annual family day at a popular amusement park. The morning had started off normally; the sun was shining and the kids were excited. Now, suddenly, because of an off-handed comment from Scott about the laundry, I was being sucked into a reactive vortex.

That's when the irrational thoughts began:

Scott doesn't really love me.
We're headed for divorce.
I need to leave, right now! I can't be around him anymore.

Mustering all my self-control, I told everyone it was time to leave and went straight to the car. As we drove the forty-five minutes, I could vaguely hear the kids in the back seat speaking animatedly to each other about which attractions they were most excited about.

"I want to go on the water ride first!" exclaimed little Josie from the back seat.

I looked determinedly out the passenger side window the entire drive, trying desperately not to let the kids see the tears of frustration and anger that were falling freely now. My mind had spun out of control with the negative thoughts and I felt like I was under attack by an unseen enemy.

Arriving at the amusement park, I got out of the car without a word to anyone and surreptitiously wiped my tears, blinking rapidly to stop the flow. When we walked through the entrance, I stayed as far from my husband as possible. Teenage Gabby fell into step beside me.

"Mom, are you okay?" she asked tentatively.

"I'm fine," I lied. "I just didn't sleep well last night. I'll be okay."

I could feel her eyes on me as we walked and I tried to smile reassuringly. "I'm fine, sweetie," I insisted. "Really."

She continued to watch me for a few more minutes and then rejoined Marcus and Josie.

As we stood in line for the first ride–the water ride Josie had requested–I stayed separated from the family. With the heavy, chest-tightening anxiety suddenly weighing me down, I knew it was going to be impossible to interact in any meaningful, genuine way with anyone. My children were even taking turns to come give me hugs and ask if I was all right. Each time I continued to assure them I was fine.

Then I had a realization dawn on me: *You are going to ruin this entire day for everyone. You need to do something, now.*

The internal negative thoughts kept insisting that this wasn't my fault and that *I* didn't need to do a thing: it was Scott's fault and *he* needed to apologize. But beneath that lie I put forth the effort to dig out the painful truth: the reality was that I needed to take charge of how *I* was feeling and the reaction I was having in my body.

You need to practice your mindfulness, whispered a calm, firm voice in my mind. I was nine years into the healing portion of my journey, and had been learning to practice mindfulness meditation over the previous year. I suddenly knew this was the answer to my predicament. It was time to put my new tool into action. I excused myself, telling Scott I needed a little bit of time alone.

"Okay," was his brief reply.

Wandering the crowded amusement park for ten minutes, I finally found a bench tucked away in a corner off the busy thoroughfare and began the meditation.

Sitting in an upright position on the bench with my hands resting on my knees and my gaze soft, resting on the ground in front of me, I began to focus on my breath. *Just this breath coming in . . . just this breath going out.* At first, my angry mind resisted like a toddler throwing a tantrum. But I persisted, knowing that pushback was part of the process. *Just this breath coming in . . . just this breath going out.*

As my mind kept trying to drag my thoughts back to the comment Scott had made and the spiral that led my mind to conclude we were doomed for divorce, I acknowledged those thoughts and then gently but firmly guided my mind back to my breathing.

Just this breath coming in . . . just this breath going out.

After a few minutes, I felt myself grounded in the present thanks to those steady, smooth inhales and exhales. Next, I mentally began to explore my body. First, I noted tightness in my chest and allowed myself to observe the sensation without judgment, breathing fully into my chest and out again.

I had learned that each sensation–like emotions–were not inherently good or bad, they were just doing a job and delivering information. When I viewed them with curiosity instead of judgment, the sensations could deliver their message and usually passed soon after.

After a few moments, I continued through the rest of my body, recognizing a tingling in my fingers. I observed the feeling with curiosity, then imagined my breath flowing into my fingertips and back out again. As I addressed each part of my body, the uncomfortable sensations and harsh emotions related to them began to relax. The anger and anxiety ebbed gently away.

When ten minutes of mindfulness practice had passed, I looked up again and found myself feeling at peace. I sat for a few minutes more, simply watching the people walking nearby. I noticed the warmth of the sun and the smell of popcorn in the air. I arose with a sense of gratitude. I returned to my family and apologized to Scott.

Hugging me warmly, he replied, "I'm really sorry for making that stupid comment this morning. I was just feeling irritated."

"I know. I don't think my reaction really had anything to do with you," I confided. "I think it triggered something in me that needs to be processed with my therapist."

He simply nodded, knowing that I had my own answers these days, and he trusted my intuition.

The rest of the day was beautiful. We had so much fun as a family! Together, we enjoyed riding rides, playing silly games with each other as we waited in line, eating yummy, unhealthy park food, and watching performances from local music groups.

As we drove home that night in the dark, I held Scott's hand. I looked over at him and he glanced back, smiling and squeezing my hand lovingly. I turned to look at my children, all fast asleep. My heart swelled with gratitude for the gift that mindfulness had given me that day. I was able to take back control when old wounds tried to hijack my mind and body. *I'm so thankful that today is a happy memory for us all*, I thought as I turned back around. I leaned my seat back and closed my eyes.

Mastering Mindfulness

Living with bipolar symptoms for years, I'd felt like a victim to intense emotions and negative, intrusive thoughts that bombarded my mind. I hated being in my own head and developed a habit of intentionally daydreaming in an attempt to escape the chaos in my brain.

Once I was off of medication and micronutrients helped my brain heal, I began to gain more control. I used my Mood Cycle Survival Guide, and went to therapy to become more aware of triggers and thought patterns that caused symptoms of hypomania, depression, and anxiety. The challenge was that awareness of my particular triggers wasn't sufficient to stop all of my reactions.

I had heard about mindfulness meditation from various sources but did not really understand what it was or its value as a healing tool. Then one day, I read a post on social media from a high school friend. He shared how mindfulness meditation had helped him overcome debilitating depression and anxiety brought on by a traumatic divorce.

I purchased the book he referred to, *Mindfulness: An Eight-week Plan for Finding Peace in a Frantic World*, by Mark Williams and Danny Penman. Early on, this passage caught my attention:

"When there is something to be scared or stressed about—whether real or imagined—our ancient 'fight-or-flight' reactions kick in as they should. But then something else happens: the mind begins to trawl through memories to try and find something that will explain why we are feeling like this . . .The result is that the brain's alarm signals start to be triggered not only by the current scare, but by past threats and future worries. This happens in an instant, before we're even aware of it." (Williams, Mark and Danny Penman. *Mindfulness: An Eight-week Plan for Finding Peace in a Frantic World.*)

A lightbulb went on for me. I realized the pattern of mental triggers that propelled me into fight or flight mode and reactions that were out of proportion to each current situation. I decided to learn how to practice mindfulness meditation to:

- Create a greater awareness of what was happening in my mind and
- Learn how to stay present rather than allowing my mind to drag me helplessly into the past or future.

"You can't stop the triggering of unhappy memories, negative self-talk and judgmental ways of thinking—but what you can stop is what happens next. You can stop the vicious circle from feeding off itself and triggering the next spiral of negative thoughts. And you can do this by harnessing an alternative way of relating to yourself and the world." (Williams, Mark and Danny Penman. *Mindfulness: An Eight-week Plan for Finding Peace in a Frantic World.*)

My initial attempts with their eight-week program resulted in a few false starts. Because I wasn't fully committed, I would sporadically do the guided meditations prescribed in the book. What I noticed was profound: a feeling of being more grounded and self-aware on the days I *practiced*. Finally, on a cold day in January, I committed myself fully to the eight-week plan outlined in the book.

The program consists of reading a specific chapter at the beginning of the week, followed by guided meditations morning and night. I practiced my boundaries by posting a sign on my bedroom door when I was meditating and let Scott and my kids know what I was doing so they wouldn't interrupt.

This experience was life changing for me. I discovered how to become friends with my mind again! Here are some of the most important benefits and insights I gained from this practice.

Grounding

The first lesson I learned was the importance of grounding yourself in the present. Many symptoms of depression and anxiety are the result of your mind or body living in the past or future. The morning of our family's amusement park adventure that summer, Scott's comment brought up feelings of distress and danger based on past events and my body was hijacked. By practicing mindfulness meditation, I was able to bring my mind and body back to the present and restore a sense of safety. Through my breathing techniques and kind observation of what was happening in my body that day, I was able to pull myself back to the here-and-now, instead of unwillingly stuck in the chaos created by unhealed trauma.

In *The Body Keeps the Score* (referenced in the previous chapter), a woman who struggled with severe PTSD from years of abuse commented *"If we notice our breath we are in the present because we can't breathe in the future or the past."* Grounding yourself in the present is powerful, healing, and puts you in the driver's seat of your mind and body, instead of being a passenger, along for a bumpy ride.

You're Not Trying to Stop Your Mind From Thinking

I spent so many years feeling like my mind was my enemy because of the ceaseless barrage of negative inner dialogue. I didn't understand how to comfortably stay present. In the early days while practicing grounding meditation, I noticed my mind constantly wandering, like a dog chasing squirrels. At first, that felt like I was failing until I learned that mindfulness is not about stopping your thoughts but rather learning to observe them and create greater awareness.

The grounding meditation taught me to focus on my breath, and then when my mind wandered, I was given permission to acknowledge where it went instead of punishing myself for not "staying on task." Then I practiced gently bringing my mind back to focusing on my breath. I learned not to judge my wandering thoughts. This changed how I viewed the workings of my mind, removing shame, and replacing it with acceptance and compassion. I developed a deep sense of gratitude for my mind and how it works so diligently to help me in so many ways.

You Are Not Your Thoughts

This concept was eye-opening for me. For years, I believed I must be a bad person because of certain thoughts that entered my mind. *Only bad people think thoughts like that*, was an ever present self-judgment that contributed to shame and guilt. Mindfulness practice taught me how to *observe* my thoughts and understand that I don't have to engage with every idea that pops into my head.

One guided meditation that I practiced in the eight-week program invited me to consider my mind as a river and my thoughts as objects floating in the current. I was asked to imagine myself standing on the shore observing the thoughts without wading out into the swirling water to engage with them. Initially, this was extremely difficult because it never occurred to me to choose which thoughts to engage with, and each time I practiced the meditation, I found myself quickly swept away by the current of thoughts.

Over the weeks of practicing, however, I soon discovered that it was possible to observe without engaging. At my core, I wasn't permanently bound to every errant idea that went through my head. Instead, I could choose to let go of ideas that weren't healthy and supportive of my value, and embrace, cultivate, and celebrate the thoughts that were best for me.

Emotions Are Just Information

For as long as I could remember, I had developed a habit of labeling emotions as good or bad. Anger was "bad" or undesirable because I associated it with out of control outbursts and abusive behavior. As a result, when I felt anger, I judged myself as *being* a bad person. That black and white thinking, I discovered, was harmful and not true at all.

My practice taught me that emotions themselves are not good or bad; they are simply information. I learned to feel all my emotions without judgment and then *choose* what to do with the information, even the toughest ones that lay in "bad" categories that I was renaming.

Mindfulness meditation enabled me to learn how to feel difficult emotions and stay present. This was especially beneficial during trauma therapy.

Creating Space to Choose

Once I got the medication out of my system and my brain began to function in a healthy way, I had to relearn how to respond rather than react when I was stressed or angry. Viktor Frankl, German psychiatrist and Holocaust survivor, teaches, *"Between stimulus and response, there is a space. In that space is our power to choose our response. In our response lies our growth and our freedom."* Mindfulness empowered me to create the mental space to make that choice. And since then, I've been able to acknowledge the things that used to upset me, let them go, and create beautiful memories instead.

Creating Greater Self-awareness

The more I practiced mindfulness, the more I became aware of the connection between thoughts and emotional reactions in the body. In my experience with Scott that I related at the beginning of the chapter, I was able to recognize that the intense emotional reaction I had to his off-handed comment about the laundry had nothing to do with him and everything to do with the deep, emotional wounding I still carried. That observation led me to seek help from my therapist in identifying and processing the trauma, ultimately eliminating the trigger and healing the trauma, long-term.

Interrupting the Feedback Loop

One of the most interesting insights I gained through mindfulness practice was learning how to interrupt the feedback loop that occurs when we experience an emotional trigger. A thought or experience can be perceived by your mind as dangerous or distressing. Your body then has a physical reaction—chest tightening, difficulty breathing, heart racing. When the mind perceives the physical reaction, it tries to form an explanation—which usually intensifies the physical response.

This feedback loop bypasses the conscious mind. As I related in the experience at the beginning of the chapter, I was aware consciously that the reaction was irrational based on the provocation, but that fact alone didn't stop the chain reaction. By engaging in mindfulness, I interrupted the feedback loop and restored rational thinking.

Mindfulness meditation is an essential self-care tool I continue to use and now encourage and teach to all of my clients. It enables us to increase self-awareness, process emotions, and nurture healing.

Mindfulness also helped me recognize the impact that trauma and mental turmoil have had, not just on my brain, but also on my body. This led me to investigate yoga, which is explored in the next chapter, as the next powerful step on the path to healing.

CHAPTER 9

STEP FIVE-YOGA:
Becoming Whole Again

I t was early fall as I approached the yoga studio in our small town in Iowa. My friend Debbie had invited me to attend yoga with her for the past couple weeks, and I was looking forward to my third class with a bit of nervous excitement.

As I entered the studio, the faint smell of jasmine and eucalyptus hung gently in the air. The room was open and welcoming with old hardwood floors and artwork from Asia decorating the walls. There was a gentle bubbling of quiet conversations from the dozen or so students waiting for the class to start. Something about the space inspired reverence from the people there. I found comfort in the fact that, no matter how old or young each of us were, we came together on equal ground for an hour to learn something new.

Bonnie, the studio owner, noticed me and welcomed me warmly. "Welcome back! We're so glad you're joining us again."

Bonnie was one of those people who seemed ageless. Although her shoulder-length, curly, bobbed chestnut hair was graying noticeably, her green eyes sparkled with youth and vitality. She was about five foot, four inches and her body was strong and lithe from years of yoga practice.

Two weeks prior, during my second class, she had shared with us about her incredible visit to India over the summer. There she had deepened her knowledge of pranayama practice, meaning breathwork and meditation, and she was excited to share what she had learned.

When she referred to her trip, I thought, *it's hard to imagine someone from little pokey Fort Madison, Iowa going to somewhere as exotic as India to study yoga.*

As I laid my mat out next to my friend, I looked around at the other people in the studio. I had always imagined yoga practitioners to be thin, young, and beautiful, wearing tight-fitting leggings and sports bras, bending themselves into pretzels—like the images I'd seen portrayed in movies and magazines. The people here today were all different body types, ages, and sexes. My favorite person I observed was an older gentleman who looked to be in his late sixties in basketball shorts and a T-shirt.

I understood from Debbie that he'd been practicing yoga for years, but he didn't seem very flexible, which I had thought was the point of yoga. His mat was surrounded by props he employed to get into the various poses during the session. He had a strap, two yoga blocks, and a folded blanket.

As I watched him with curiosity, he happened to glance in my direction and smiled warmly. I managed a sheepish smile and then looked quickly down at my own mat, feeling embarrassed at having been caught staring. Even though I had a natural tendency to be competitive, I felt comfort in knowing there wasn't a crazy, unrealistic expectation in place to look a certain way on the mat.

Bonnie invited everyone to take their places. I felt a bit anxious as I stood at the top of mine with my bare feet shoulder-distance apart. Last week Bonnie had commented on my natural flexibility. "You are like Gumby!" she'd teased good-naturedly with a twinkle in her eye. It made me even more eager to prove myself a true "yogi".

"Today I want to invite you to bring an intention of *being*, instead of *striving*," she began in her soothing, alto voice. "So often in our lives, we are constantly pushing and struggling to accomplish more, be more, gain more, and it can be exhausting and depleting."

I glanced around at the other students as they all nodded in agreement. I wasn't the only one who sometimes pushed myself beyond my limits, then.

"The focus of today's practice will be the breath. Focus on each breath coming in," she demonstrated, inhaling slowly and gently, "and each breath going out." She exhaled long and slow.

"I invite you to be present in the moment and listen to your body." Bonnie gently placed her right palm on her chest and her left palm on her abdomen. "Pay attention to what your body is telling you and listen." Her eyes settled on me with a warm smile.

"I encourage you not to push yourself into any discomfort in your poses. Instead, be present in each moment. *Be* with your breath and body."

As I listened, my overachieving mind was trying to work out how to accomplish what she was teaching. I wanted so much to be *good* at yoga.

The past two weeks during practice my mind was constantly busy, analyzing her body position in each pose and trying to achieve the same appearance. Today she was asking us not to worry about what the pose looked like, but to focus on the breath. I listened intently, determined to execute her instructions precisely.

At one point in the practice, we were in downward facing dog and Bonnie invited, "In this moment, let go of regrets from the past and your worries about the future. Be present here with each breath coming in . . ." Again, she demonstrated a long, calm breath in. "And each breath going out." She exhaled audibly and slowly.

As I followed her instructions, bent over like an inverted "V" shape, with my head hanging loose toward the mat, hands and feet planted firmly on the ground, I suddenly had a sensation of a dam breaking somewhere inside me. I could feel emotions rising up through my torso and throat and spilling out through tears onto the mat below me. As I stared through blurry vision at the rapidly growing pool beneath me, I felt confusion and alarm. *What is happening to me?*

At first, I tried to resist the tears, embarrassed by what others would think, but something inside me whispered, *let it go,* and I relaxed into the unstoppable crying. The experience was extraordinarily cathartic. The rest of that practice, I no longer cared about how perfect my poses looked, just as Bonnie instructed. Instead, I became completely immersed in my breathing and being present with what was happening in my body.

As I left the studio that day, I felt a calm, quiet sense of peace that I didn't fully understand. I realized that perhaps my 'inflexible' classmate understood something that I didn't and I wanted to discover what it was!

I wasn't able to continue with that particular yoga studio because of the expense, so I turned to yoga DVDs and later YouTube practices. Over time, I started to recognize that there were different types of yoga practice. One instructor referred to the difference as "activating" versus "restorative" yoga.

As I developed greater self-awareness through the use of my Mood Cycle Survival Guide, and therapy, I recognized that when I was experiencing depressive symptoms, I was drawn to restorative yoga. On days when I was feeling mentally more balanced, I enjoyed the challenge of activating practices.

Through mindfulness meditation, I could regularly see the impact that the turmoil in my mind was having on my body. I recognized I carried tension in my shoulders and neck, which at times caused headaches. It occurred to me that maybe there was a way to address this using yoga. I wanted my practices to be more self-directed, just like when I took the time to find the specific therapist and specific modalities to help me in another part of my healing. I often felt internal resistance to what the yoga instructor on the video was telling me to do, but I was unsure of what to do instead.

I sensed I was just brushing the surface of what was possible with yoga in my healing journey, so I began to look for books to help me gain a deeper understanding of this tool. That was when I discovered *Mental and Emotional Healing Through Yoga: A Guiding Framework for Therapists and Their Clients* by Ghada Osman, a psychotherapist and certified yoga therapist (someone specially trained to utilize yoga as a healing modality).

In the book I read:

> *"Most of us have not been trained to notice our physical sensations until they become overwhelming. Instead, we pay attention to the thought and the story. If we notice anger, we replay in our minds the argument that we had. As a result, we get ourselves more worked up as we focus on that moment in the past when the argument occurred, instead of noticing the signs of anger in the body that we have in the present."*
> (Osman, Ghada. *Mental and Emotional Healing Through Yoga.*)

In practicing mindfulness, I was already becoming more conscious of what was happening in my mind; however, I only noticed physical sensations when I was doing a guided meditation or when they became overwhelming. Just as mindfulness had helped me to become friends with my mind again, I realized that yoga could help me powerfully and effectively integrate my mind *and* body.

Integrating Mind and Body

I recognized that in my efforts to heal my "mental illness," a disconnect had occurred. I had begun to view my mind as separate from my body, and that fragmentation was hindering my progression along that path to healing.

"Talk of 'the mind–body connection' implies that we are linking two separate things, as if the mind were distinct from, rather than a part of, the body. Even though we can acknowledge that illness in much of the body tends to be accompanied by low spirits and cognitive dullness, and that physical activity is key in supporting emotional health, for some reason we still evaluate emotional health separately from other realms of physical health." (Osman, Ghada. *Mental and Emotional Healing Through Yoga.*)

Integrating my mind and body through yoga helped me understand the relationship between my thoughts, feelings, and physical sensations. I learned to interpret the messages my body was giving me, and see all parts of myself, including my emotions, as valid and worthy of acknowledgement. I had already begun some of this from my mindfulness practice, so what I was now learning both in books and in yoga itself was aligning beautifully.

Feeling Rather Than Resisting Emotions

When I was reading *The Body Keeps the Score*, I found a chapter on yoga as a healing modality.

"The lives of many trauma survivors come to revolve around bracing against and neutralizing unwanted sensory experiences . . . When people are chronically angry or scared, constant muscle tension ultimately leads to spasms, back pain, migraine headaches, fibromyalgia and other forms of chronic pain. They may visit multiple specialists, undergo extensive diagnostic tests, and be prescribed multiple medications, some of which may provide temporary relief but all of which

fail to address the underlying issues." (Van der Kolk, Bessel. *The Body Keeps the Score.*)

Yoga is a mindfulness exercise that creates awareness around the sensations in your body and helps you recognize when you are resisting emotions instead of allowing yourself to feel them. Remember how I gave myself permission to feel what broke through during that third yoga class with Bonnie? This can give you additional clues for working with your therapist and processing past trauma or issues.

"Simply noticing what you feel fosters emotional regulation, and it helps you to stop trying to ignore what is going on inside you. As I often tell my students, the two most important phrases in therapy, as in yoga, are 'Notice that' and 'What happens next?' Once you start approaching your body with curiosity rather than fear, everything shifts." (Van der Kolk, Bessel. *The Body Keeps the Score.*)

There is power in allowing yourself to move through emotions instead of resisting them. It lets your mind know that the emotion has done its job and then allows it to dissipate like mist in the morning sun.

One of the blessings that came from this new awareness was recognition of the tension that I was constantly holding in my chest and shoulders. As I nourished my body through consistent yoga practice and noticed the tension without judgment, I found the rigidity calmed down and the headaches went away!

Confidence

When I first started practicing yoga, I was very focused on doing it correctly. I was critically concerned with how I looked on the outside. As I gained a deeper understanding of yoga, however, I discovered it is truly about connecting more fully and completely with yourself. What was more important than flawless form was feeling gratitude for my incredible body and everything it does for me each day. Accepting yourself *fully as you are* is one of the keys to confidence.

Yoga practice helps cultivate appreciation for your whole self, exactly as you are in the moment. That fact first took root in Bonnie's studio when I saw the different ages, sizes, and skill levels of the other students. I also saw it more on YouTube videos at home, where I learned from all kinds of people how to embrace that inner value more than just what lay on the surface outside.

As time went by and I improved my balance and strength, I gained confidence in my ability to persevere in challenging situations in other aspects of my life. Learning how to sit with discomfort, whether it was emotions or poses, increased my self-assurance to handle the challenges of daily life with greater equanimity and poise.

You Can Only Breathe in the Present

Breathing is generally something we do without thinking. In yoga, breath is a *primary* consideration. You are asked to notice your breath, are given prescribed breath patterns in pranayama practice, and are often invited to breathe in and out in rhythm as you move through poses. This helps ground you in the present and more fully integrate your mind and body.

Yoga and its accompanying breathwork has been claimed for over 2,500 years as restorative and healing to the body and mind. Deep breathing has been clinically shown to release toxins and improve the quality of your blood, improve mood, release tension, increase brain clarity, relieve pain, strengthen your immune system, strengthen the heart and lungs, as well as improve stamina and cellular regeneration. (Nestor, James. *Breath.*) It's a healing modality all its own—inside of our own bodies!

Osman's Three-Pronged Model

I noticed that depending on my mental or emotional state, I gravitated toward specific types of yoga and felt stressed or agitated by other postures and practices. According to Osman, in addition to activating and restorative yoga, there is grounding practice as well. Understanding how the different types of yoga impact your mental state helps you identify which approach best serves your needs. She refers to this as the Three-Pronged model.

Grounding

Grounding poses helped me feel a sense of safety and stability in the present moment. It deepened my experience of grounding with mindfulness meditation by engaging my entire body in the process. It is important to begin any yoga practice with grounding. If you find yourself becoming stressed or agitated, you can return to a grounding pose to reestablish your emotional equilibrium.

> *"Grounding emphasizes balance and evenness . . . this means maintaining straight lines, symmetry, and contact with the floor on both sides of the body. . . it means maintaining the same breath count on the inhale and exhale, and breathing in and out through the nose."* (Osman, Ghada. *Mental and Emotional Healing Through Yoga.*)

My favorite grounding poses are mountain, downward facing dog, and child's pose. If I am dealing with especially high levels of stress, I will have the urge to go into downward facing dog or child's pose during my yoga sessions. I understand now that my body is asking to be grounded in that moment and it is vital to my success that I listen.

Activating (Brahmana)

I found this type of practice served me best when I was feeling emotionally balanced and healthy. I loved the challenge of an activating practice to invigorate my mind and body.

> *"[Postures] that encourage brahmana energy may include back movement in the spine, movement in the hips, and invigorating flow between movements . . . breathing that increases brahmana includes breaths with a long inhale and a rapid, more forceful exhale."* (Osman, Ghada. *Mental and Emotional Healing Through Yoga.*)

Some of my favorite activating practices involve balancing poses, core work, and flowing quickly from one pose to the next. These practices are energizing. The more I progressed on my healing journey, the greater my desire to engage in activating yoga practices—they felt empowering and were also more physically challenging, which I found very useful to my health at those times.

Restorative (Langhana)

Restorative yoga is beneficial for helping me relax my mind and body when I feel agitated, anxious, or stressed.

> *"Yoga [postures] and breathing that promote langhana relax the body, reduce the heart rate, stimulate the parasympathetic nervous system, and calm the mind. [Postures] that encourage langhana include forward bends and restorative styles, while . . . breathing includes breaths with a longer exhale than inhale."* (Osman, Ghada. *Mental and Emotional Healing Through Yoga.*)

My favorite restorative pose is the forward bend. It seems simple, but I can feel the tension in my body drain away as I ground my lower body and relax forward—as if it drains out of my fingertips into the ground.

Listening to Your Body to Facilitate Healing

Treating my body and mind as one unit and learning how to listen and nourish my whole self through yoga has been a powerful resource for healing. Some of those moments have been during an activating practice because I was ready for a mental and physical challenge to improve confidence and resilience. Others were moments when I was doing healing work with my therapist or experiencing excessive stress in my life that were best served through grounding or restorative practices.

I have frequently heard people say, "I tried yoga but didn't like it." I've discovered upon further inquiry that often what they mean is they went to a yoga class and the type of yoga in that class didn't serve their mental or emotional state at the time. This is why I have incorporated simple, informative education on utilizing yoga for healing in my coaching program. Yoga is such a powerful healing modality if it is understood and implemented properly.

My increased self-awareness also helped me understand the vital importance of caring for myself physically as I work to restore mental health. I further realized that I needed to incorporate daily exercise in my overall health and wellness routine, which we will discuss in the next chapter. Over the last twelve years, I have noticed a miraculous difference.

CHAPTER 10

STEP SIX-EXERCISE:
Run For Your Life

Lightning flashed, followed quickly by thunder so intense that a few car alarms went off in the parking lot of our apartment complex in Mississippi. I had just stepped outside, bicycle in tow, to do my training ride. My heart raced with the shock of the sudden sound and I stood still for a moment, afraid to move. The fear quickly turned to exasperation as I realized that I couldn't safely ride in this weather. Turning around, I stalked back into the apartment and yanked the sliding door open to roughly return my bike back to the porch.

Scott walked out of the bedroom when he heard me slam the door. "What's up?" he asked, his face full of concern.

"This is the fourth day I haven't been able to train and I'm so frustrated!" I said, collapsing onto the couch and wrapping my arms tightly around my body.

Scott sat next to me and put his arm around me. "I can understand that. I've noticed how much regular exercise has been helping you these past couple months since you decided to do the triathlon," he commented gently.

"Well, it's not helping me today, is it?" I retorted.

We sat in silence for a few minutes before I could feel Scott looking at me. Finally, I turned and demanded, "What?"

Scott paused before asking, "Are you open to an observation?"

Those were the magic words that signaled to me Scott wanted to help but didn't want to have his head bitten off. It wouldn't work. "Not right now," I answered honestly. "I'm too upset."

Accepting my reply, Scott calmly sat with me for a few more minutes before finally getting up and returning to our bedroom. I remained fuming on the couch for a few more minutes before curiosity overcame my discouragement and I followed Scott into the bedroom.

"What is your observation?" I asked in a now measured tone.

Glancing up from his computer, his eyes gentle, he responded, "Remember, this is not criticism or judgment, just an observation."

I nodded my silent assent and he continued.

"Over the past few months since you started exercising consistently, I've noticed that you are happier and able to handle stress much better." After a brief hesitation, he added, "I don't think that exercise is just something *nice* for you to do; I think it's *necessary* for your mental health. I don't think it's optional."

In the silence, I could see my husband bracing himself for an angry reply, but it didn't come. Instead, I left my mind open and let the truth of his words settle in. I really had been happier for a long period when I was able to experience daily–or nearly daily–exercise. My level of frustration today was testament of what happened when I was prevented from participating in it for too many days in a row. Sitting down on the bed, I started to cry. "I know," I sighed meekly. "I've noticed the same thing."

Once again, Scott came and sat by me, putting his arm comfortingly around me. "I'm not saying that to make you feel bad," he reassured me. "I want to help. What can I do?"

Against the backdrop of lightning, thunder, and rain pelting the windows, we spent the next half hour discussing the different things that had prevented me from working out that week–staying up late watching shows, becoming distracted by a project and of course the weather–and what I could do to prioritize exercise in my day. By the time we were done, I was feeling more calm and even excited by some of the ideas we had come up with together.

Scott and I both recognized the mental health benefits of regular exercise—greater ability to handle stress, elevated mood from the endorphins, better sleep quality, and better focus and mental clarity.

Triggering Symptoms with Training?

When I started on the micronutrients and my brain began to wake up, I had a desire to improve my overall health. After all, I'd been working hard on understanding and integrating the mind/body connection into my wellness journey, so challenging myself with a new fitness routine seemed like the perfect step alongside the ones I'd taken for my mind.

I decided to start exercising regularly, and as a former competitive athlete, the only way I knew to exercise was to train for a specific goal. When I was a swim coach back in Fort Madison, I had adult triathletes ask me for help with their swimming technique, which piqued my interest in triathlons.

Shortly after moving to Mississippi, I found a local sprint triathlon to sign up for, bought two books on triathlon training, made a workout plan, and got to work. I was all about getting "better" overall, and at first, this new plan worked out beautifully for me.

When I completed the triathlon a few months later, I was exhilarated by the competition. "I forgot how much I love to compete!" I exclaimed after crossing the finish line. The last time I'd felt anything like this was back on the swim team in college! Unfortunately, in the weeks following the event, I found myself getting mildly depressed, struggling to keep exercising without a specific goal to work toward.

I just need to find something new to train for, I thought and began looking for my next race. Over the following five years, I developed a pattern of signing up for events—triathlons or road races, including the Mama Bear 5k that I did just four months following Josie's birth, pushing her in the stroller. I never let grass grow under my feet. However, through the use of my Mood Cycle Survival Guide, I started to see a pattern.

When I trained for events, I would experience some mild symptoms of hypomania: slightly elevated mood, racing thoughts and ideas, and a desire to take on more projects. After I completed the event, I would experience mild depressive symptoms: struggling to focus, fatigue, and feeling overwhelmed by whatever new projects I had taken on during the upswing.

This was a paradox for me: I could definitely see the benefits of exercise, but my *approach* was triggering a mood swing that I knew could become a big problem. I puzzled over this dilemma. Then one day, after two triathlons and five road races, I had an experience that began to shift my perspective.

Why is it so hard to get up off the couch and do my run today? I thought, exasperated with myself. I was supposed to go on a five-mile tempo run for my triathlon training, and this time the weather wasn't even an excuse to not get off my butt; outside, the sun was shining and the temperature was just right. But I had been procrastinating for an hour now, watching YouTube videos of professional triathletes racing instead of going on my own run.

I usually looked forward to my training and the wonderful endorphins and other benefits I got from exercise, but today was one of those days I had occasionally, when just the idea of pushing myself physically seemed exhausting in itself.

I had been noticing that on the days when I felt like this, the exercise almost made me feel worse—draining my emotional, physical, and mental resources instead of replenishing them. As I considered my predicament, a new idea crossed my mind. What if instead of *making* myself do the scheduled run, I took off my watch that I used for pacing and ran just for the fun of it?

Part of me felt like that would be cheating. *What's the matter with you? Those professional athletes know how to push themselves on the days when they don't feel like training!*

But another part of me encouraged the unexplored concept. *You're not a professional athlete, Michelle. And doing something is better than doing nothing.*

Finally, I decided to go for it. Not allowing myself time to second-guess, I quickly took off my watch, set it on the counter, and walked out the door. As I started to run, I struggled at first with some mental discomfort. I had to laugh because I was used to checking my pace. Automatically, I kept glancing down at regular intervals only to remember that I wasn't wearing my watch.

Gradually, however, I began to shake off the old routine and actually notice things around me. It was May and the air was warm, and slightly humid, but with a comfortable breeze. The trees were bright green with new leaves and filled with the sound of birds. Normally, I would be too concerned with the numbers needed to make the run "successful" to notice such details.

I settled into what felt like a comfortable pace, even smiling and waving at cars as they passed me on the road. At an intersection, I decided to take the gravel road, thinking fondly of the poem, *The Road Not Taken*, by Robert Frost. A half mile down the road, I chuckled out loud when I startled a cow in a pasture that took off running across the field. At the next intersection, I opted to turn right toward the park. It certainly wasn't the path I usually took, but my feet kept jogging along and my breath was even as I experienced this lively, newfound freedom.

As I drew nearer to the park, I could hear the *thwack* of a baseball being hit and the shouts of a Little League crowd cheering. *This is like a choose your own adventure run*, I thought exuberantly to myself as I decided to turn left at the next intersection, even though that meant I'd run up a steep hill for a full quarter of a mile.

When I arrived home forty-five minutes later, I had no idea how far I had run, but I felt emotionally rejuvenated, even though I was physically tired! It would be a few more years before I really understood what happened on that run that day.

Why Run?

That triathlon was the last time I signed up for a race. As much as I loved competing, I valued my mental health more. Somehow I needed to find a way to benefit my body and my mind at the same time. On the day back in Mississippi when Scott and I brainstormed ideas for exercising more consistently, one idea had been to join a gym, so I decided to try signing up for exercise classes at a local recreation center.

At first, I really enjoyed the social aspect, but it could at times be a double-edged sword. Some days I didn't want to be around people, and my choice was to force myself to be social or skip my exercise altogether. I also found that on days when I was struggling emotionally, the extra step of driving to the gym could prove a barrier to following through. And then there was the monthly expense of the membership fee to consider while our family was still growing.

I tried swimming, which I had loved most of my life, but again, it was a much greater commitment of time and money. I realized that during high school, my regular swim training probably mitigated a lot of symptoms without me knowing it! Yet, the last time I tried swimming regularly, the recreation center was shut down because of the pandemic. The irony in that was that at a time when I really needed to exercise to manage stress, the facility that I was depending on for my exercise was closed.

That was when I committed fully to running and walking as my foundational form of exercise. They were simple, inexpensive, and accessible.

Simple: Just put your shoes on and walk out the door. Most people can at least walk, and running is easier than you think if you work up to it gently and gradually.

Inexpensive: No monthly fees or fancy equipment, just a supportive pair of shoes.

Accessible: You don't need a gym or to drive anywhere and you can exercise even when traveling.

I always encourage anyone focused on healing their mental health to consider making walking or running the foundational piece of their exercise plan. If you enjoy other forms of exercise–workout classes, weight lifting, cycling, etc.–by all means participate in them. But keep a thirty-minute, three times a week, walk or run as part of your routine. This gives you a stable, sustainable, more mild form of exercise that will support your mental health no matter your location or circumstances. Now, thirteen years into my healing journey, I use exercise regularly. It has made a huge difference.

Focusing on Exercise for Mental Health, Not Weight Loss

During the two-year period when Scott was out of work, the prolonged stress caused me to gain weight. When we moved to Utah for his new job, I started focusing on exercise for weight loss. I began weighing myself daily and when the pounds didn't go away, I started feeling discouraged. The focus of my running became about my physical appearance and not my mental health—and the result was my mental health suffered.

Since my runs were not enjoyable anymore, I finally quit. A few months later, however, I saw someone running and had an overwhelming desire to go on a run. I really missed the benefits of consistent, daily exercise.

I mulled over everything I had learned over the previous years about how exercise impacted my mental health. I threw away my scale and created a plan going forward that focused primarily on benefitting my mental health; everything else fell into place. My weight dropped naturally because I was releasing and eliminating tremendous stress.

Building Mental and Physical Stamina

When I first started running, I discovered quickly how important it was to start from square one. No matter how strong I thought I was, without being a steady runner for a long time, I had to work my way up gradually. It was important to start small, with short walks and jogs, and build gradually.

I developed a twelve-week plan that eventually led to completing a thirty-minute run. It was important physically to increase incrementally to build physical stamina and prevent injury. The gradual progression also increased my *mental* stamina to handle that length of consistent physical exertion. I found that stamina translated into my daily life, giving me greater confidence and resilience to meet challenges.

Keeping Promises to Myself

In addition to stamina, I began gaining confidence in myself when I followed through on workout plans. I was prioritizing my self-care in order to stay healthy and balanced mentally. Each time I followed through on a workout, it increased my confidence.

Self-discipline had been something I struggled with for years because of my mood swings. But over time, as my brain healed, I discovered the things that drove me forward and worked well to ensure my success. I was able to stay more stable and followed through on my self-care routine. Those personal wins increased my feelings of self-worth and confidence.

Get Out and Move

There were some days when I would have low emotional resources, like that day I mentioned earlier when it just felt like exercising would do more harm than its usual good. This was especially true when I was working through healing trauma or other triggers in therapy.

During those periods, I recognized that I struggled more to get out and run.

I knew that it was important to exercise, but perhaps running wasn't right at that time. On those days, I opted to just go on a walk. Walking was easier to face mentally and still got me outside and moving, which was the goal and I always felt better afterward.

On days when exercising outside simply wasn't an option–perhaps due to bad weather–I was able to utilize an activating yoga routine to get my heart rate up.

Injury Prevention

Injury prevention became a top priority for me as over the years I experienced a few setbacks of my own when I occasionally got hurt. Although you can't prevent every injury, there are some tips that can help avoid many common issues.

First, invest in sturdy, well-fitting shoes. I found it was beneficial to go to a running store and be fitted for the right shoes. The first pair were the most expensive because I purchased them directly from the store, but once I found the right brand, size, and style, I looked for sales and would replace them at a significant discount. Having great shoes helped eliminate many of the causes of typical running injuries.

Second, stretching and strengthening are paramount. I found that with yoga I could "kill two birds with one stone." I found routines that helped me to stretch, to strengthen, and protect my body and mind at the same time. This simplified my self-care significantly and I found it helped me stay injury free.

Third, don't overdo it. Some people think if a little exercise is good, a lot is better, but that isn't necessarily true. Focusing on consistent, moderate exercise can help prevent your body from getting overstressed and injured.

Exercising Outside

Being outside in fresh air and sunshine gives added benefits to the exercise. One study showed that, *"Exercise outside at the same time every day . . . will help keep your brain time aligned with real time so you can fall asleep faster."* (Heisz, Jennifer. *Move the Body, Heal the Mind.*)

This was absolutely the case for me! I have experimented with different times of day for exercise and my favorite is first thing in the morning. Stepping outside into the fresh air and getting my heart rate up is an invigorating way to start my day. At night, when my head hits the pillow, I am out and I sleep well through the night, waking up refreshed and ready for a new day.

There are also incredible, psychological benefits to witnessing the change of seasons, and the cyclical nature of plants, animals, and creation that, while simple, can be absolutely profound in terms of understanding the world and recognizing our special place in it. I even developed a love for running in frigid winter temperatures—the cold air really wakes me up!

Mindfulness

Initially when I started running outside, I didn't wear headphones for safety reasons, since I exercised alone. When I started practicing mindfulness, I was astonished to recognize that running outside without headphones gave me similar benefits of mindfulness meditation!

Often when I tell people that I run without earbuds, they respond, "Oh, I could never do that! Exercise is too boring!" But that discomfort in our own bodies with what we are doing is the very thing that we are trying to repair with mindfulness and yoga. Learning to stay *present* in your body while running or walking is extremely important.

As you can probably tell by now, I have a very active mind. The things that have helped me not be bored during running or walking are:

- Focusing on my breath and experimenting with different breathing patterns, similar to what I learned in yoga. My favorite breath pattern is breathing in for three steps and out for two.
- Doing running drills and focusing on my form. This is actually really fun. You can look up YouTube videos on running drills and do them as part of your warm-up. Then pay attention to your form while you run. This will help you become more efficient in your movement and can help prevent injury too!
- It can be fun to count how many steps you take in sixty seconds on

regular terrain. Then how many uphill or downhill.

- I also found that as I am running or walking, if I smile and wave at cars and people I pass, I get an extra boost. I don't care if they smile or wave back—in my mind everyone is either a friend or a potential friend. This habit gives me the benefits of being social and smiling makes me feel happier. That's been scientifically proven too! *"When you smile, your brain releases dopamine, endorphins and serotonin. These neurotransmitters are associated with lowering your anxiety and increasing feelings of happiness. In fact, serotonin is often the chemical that antidepressant medications attempt to regulate."*[7]

EMDR While Running?

I began noticing that when I was struggling with a challenge in my life, my brain would process it while I ran. Frequently, I came up with inspiration for solving the issue. When I mentioned this phenomena to Shirley in a therapy session, she responded, "Yes, that's actually how EMDR was discovered in the first place. The founder of EMDR recognized that her eye movement while she was walking in the park allowed her to process distressing memories and this led her to the discovery of the modality."

What an incredible revelation! I loved learning that my mind was naturally engaging in EMDR during a run. No wonder I often felt mentally, emotionally, and physically better afterwards.

Healing Mental Illness with Exercise

In her book, *Move the Body, Heal the Mind,* Dr. Jennifer Heisz shares some additional insight into the benefits of exercise in helping heal mental illness. She discusses studies that have proven exercise to be more effective than antidepressants at treating depression: *"A review of twenty-seven studies with over 1,400 clinically depressed adults revealed antidepressant effects from both aerobic and strength exercise interventions."* (Heisz, Jennifer. *Move the*

---

[7] www.aultman.org/blog/caring-for-you/world-smile-day-how-smiling-affects-your-brain/#/.

Body, Heal the Mind.)

It felt validating to see this in black and white, since Scott had made a similar observation when I began my regular fitness routine—not to mention what happened when I wasn't able to get my scheduled workouts in.

Exercise helps us to handle stress more effectively. *"Now, you're physically stronger and can push your body faster and harder than ever before. You're also mentally stronger and less reactive to everyday stressors . . . Exercise is the medicine that we all need."* (Heisz, Jennifer. *Move the Body, Heal the Mind.*)

In the immortal words of Elle Woods from the movie, *Legally Blonde* (2001), *"Exercise gives you endorphins. Endorphins make you happy."* Daily running has become one of my favorite parts of my self-care routine. I love being outside running, walking, or hiking even, paying attention to the world around me and staying present with myself in the moment.

There were times when stressful moves, illness, or other circumstances caused me to stop running for long enough periods of time that I needed to "start over" with my twelve-week plan. I learned not to view this as failure or with discouragement. Each time I would do a "reset," I would remind myself, *you know how to do this. You've done it before.* And away I would go.

It turned out this was a mindset that benefited me in the bipolar healing process in general. The mindset necessary for healing will be discussed in the next chapter.

CHAPTER 11

STEP SEVEN-MINDSET FOR HEALING:
The Path to Healing Is NOT Linear . . .
But It Does Exist

I'd like to continue to be real with you: some weeks, the mountain of recovery was easier to climb than others. I loved being able to see tangible results. Those results meant life was not only doable but much more enjoyable. The beautiful empowerment I felt compelled me to take more steps. However, being goal-oriented, I had imagined myself climbing a peak toward mental wellness and balance. Unfortunately, that mental image meant that each time I experienced symptoms, no matter how mild, it felt like stumbling back down the trail—like a game of chutes and ladders. If I "landed" on a circumstance that triggered symptoms and caused me to slide backward on that path, it felt like failure to me because I wanted so much to reach my destination of "healed."

Every so often, I found myself in Shirley's office, frustrated by a bout of depression that weighed me down. She was always there for me, and, one summer afternoon after three full months without symptoms, she gave me one of her compassionate smiles.

"The path to healing is not linear," Shirley shared gently. "It looks more like the addiction recovery cycle. Are you familiar with that?"

"No, I'm not," I replied.

Shirley picked up her small whiteboard that she often used to explain concepts and began to draw as she explained: "In addiction recovery, there are stages that indicate your mindset and choices." She wrote *precontemplation*, *contemplation*, *determination*, *action*, *maintenance*, and *learning points* in a circle on the board with arrows between each word.

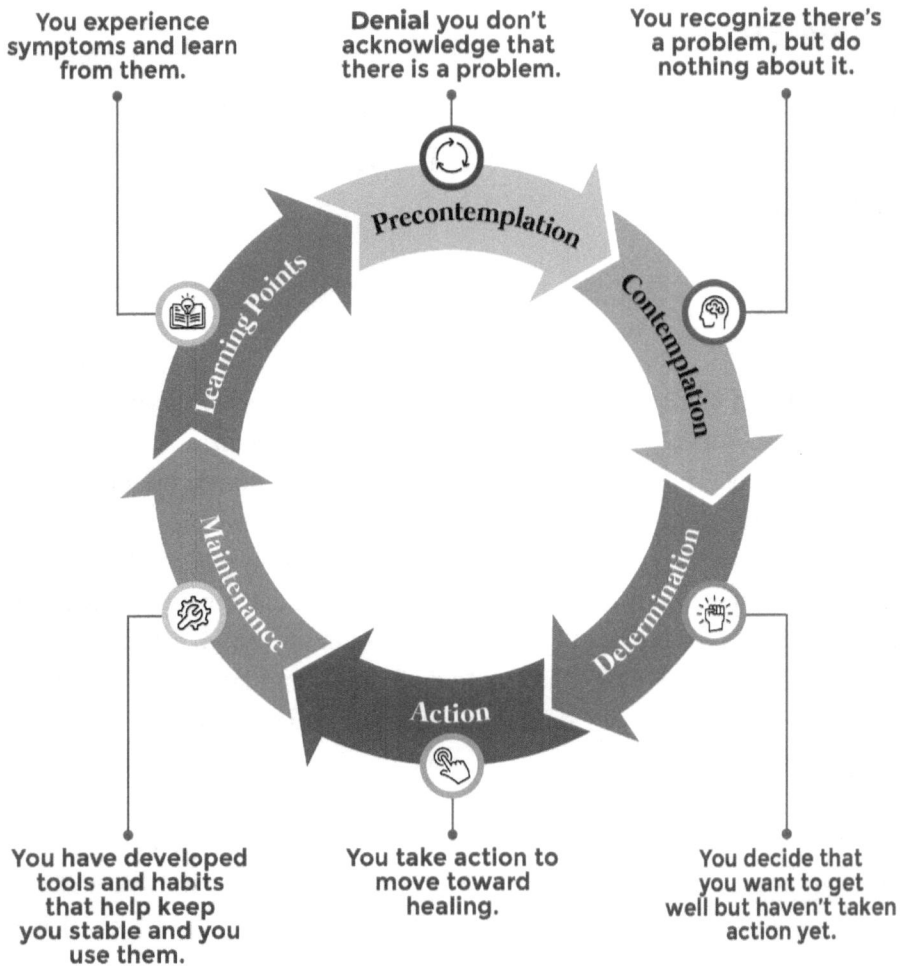

You experience symptoms and learn from them.

Denial you don't acknowledge that there is a problem.

You recognize there's a problem, but do nothing about it.

You have developed tools and habits that help keep you stable and you use them.

You take action to move toward healing.

You decide that you want to get well but haven't taken action yet.

"The goal, Michelle, is to eliminate *precontemplation* and *contemplation* from the cycle." Shirley put lines through each word as she said them. "And stay here, moving through ***determination, action, maintenance,*** and ***learning points***.

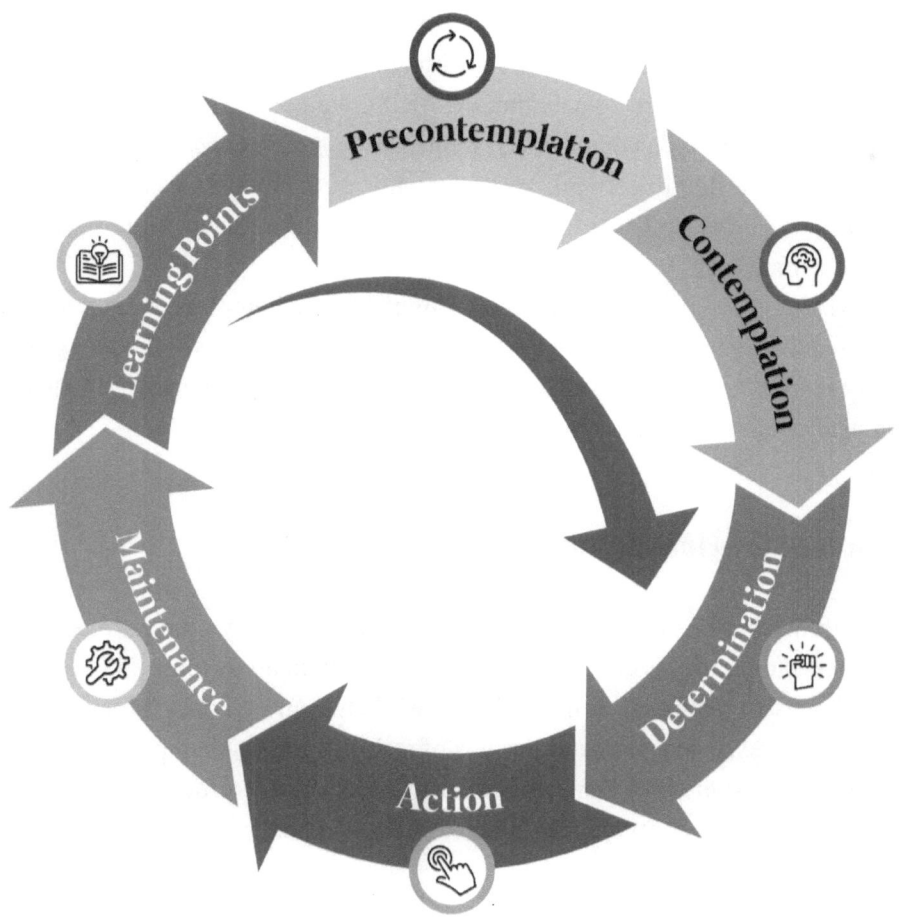

"You don't forget what you have learned and done in the action stage and so it becomes easier to return to maintenance much more quickly. Eventually, you experience fewer learning points where you may feel triggered, and you spend longer periods of time here," she said, pointing to maintenance.

As I considered what Shirley was sharing, it all fit together and came into focus.

Oh my goodness! I've been thinking about this all wrong!

A wave of relief rushed through my body as the depth of this realization filled me to my very core. I had been living this recovery cycle the past ten years without even realizing it. It all started with eliminating the medication and beginning to heal with the micronutrients. The Mood Cycle Survival Guide (MCSG) had been key. Even though I didn't use the specific terms Shirley was describing, I knew that the MCSG helped me be aware of *learning points* and to focus on *action* to return me to *maintenance*.

"This is so helpful! Thank you!" I finally exclaimed. "I wish I'd understood this sooner so I wouldn't have felt like a failure every time I experienced symptoms."

When I arrived home, I headed straight for my computer and created a visual depiction of the "recovery cycle." I put it up on my wall. It was a great, daily reminder to me that relapse was not failure and to help me stay focused on healing and recovery.

Mindset for Healing and Recovery

Identifying and healing the underlying causes of bipolar symptoms takes time and persistence. My journey that I shared with you in all its messy, honest ups and downs is proof that ultimately life gets better, more beautiful, and more joyful. You experience greater periods of stability without symptoms.

There are some important principles to understand in order to be successful and I'd like to continue sharing them with you here.

You Never Start From Zero

Oliver Wendell Holmes, Jr. is credited with saying, *"Man's mind, once stretched by a new idea, never regains its original dimensions."* The same can be said with new tools and skills. When I felt like I was starting all over every time I experienced symptoms, I was mistaken. Each time I stumbled on that mental mountain path–a learning point–I gained much greater knowledge and experience than I had possessed before. I was actually getting stronger.

Finally, I stopped viewing those moments as failures and focused instead on learning and simply asking vital questions—but without the shame and judgment of the past. Was there a trigger or something that contributed to causing the symptoms to occur? Was I under greater stress and needed to increase my nutrient intake? Did I need to reevaluate my self-care routine?

I also became more of an expert in utilizing the MCSG and other tools—micronutrients, therapy, mindfulness meditation, yoga, and exercise—to manage and recover more quickly, and to my delight, I did! I came to see so solidly that symptoms are not indications of a "disorder"; they are simply *information* from the mind and body that there is distress that needs to be addressed, just like all humans face. Removing that shameful, negative connotation is a firm foundation for you as a person, empowering you to have what you need to move forward.

Managing Emotional Resources

During your healing process, there will be times when you have limited emotional resources. It is essential to identify your priorities in order of importance. Step Three in the MCSG—Power Priorities—played a key role in recognizing this for myself. Times when this continued to be especially applicable was when I was doing healing work in therapy with Shirley and when my family and I experienced the normal but major stressors in our life like moves or job loss.

It was necessary then to be very clear about what I was choosing to prioritize and set healthy boundaries around my emotional resources in order to facilitate healing and recovery.

As a reminder, under times of duress, keep priorities simple. My suggestion is to limit yourself to three because that is doable.

My priorities, in specific order, were **first, my self-care.** The common saying *"you have to put on your oxygen mask first before you can help anyone else"* became especially pertinent for me. Experience had shown me that if I neglected myself, everyone else suffered. The same will be true for you, so I'm sharing what I developed as a simple self-care routine that I could maintain that helped support a baseline function—no matter what was going on in my life:

Mornings (1 hour)

Brush my teeth immediately after getting up

Read 10 minutes uplifting material (scriptures)

Mindfulness meditation, prayer, bullet journaling

5 minute yoga

30 minute walk/run

5 minute yoga

Daytime (periodically throughout the day)

3 minute meditations as needed (simple deep breathing to ground you
and calm your nervous system)

Evening bedtime (15 minutes)

Brush teeth and wash face

Mindfulness meditation, prayer, bullet journaling

Sleep

Wake-up 5:00 am

Go to bed 9:00 pm

Note

I have discovered how critical a consistent sleep routine is for optimal mental
health. Going to bed early **(by 9:00 pm)** and getting up early **(by 5:00 am)**
is my daily goal.

It is important to note that this routine is "simple" for me now after years of healing and developing skills and routines. When I first started out, I would focus on one aspect at a time, making incremental adjustments as I discovered what worked best for me during different times of the day and under varying circumstances. You, as a unique being, will discover what works best for you.

My second priority was my relationship with Scott. I focused on nurturing "intentional connection" between my husband and me. Some examples are:

- Read scriptures together for ten minutes a day.
- Pray together morning and night.
- Go on inexpensive dates, sometimes just shopping together.
- Plan and enjoy movies and concerts with each other.
- Make a point of twenty-second hugs and six-second kisses each day (something we learned from Drs. John and Julie Gottman of The Gottman Institute).

These are the things that help us to stay connected to each other. My husband was, and continues to be, my number one supporter in overcoming and thriving beyond my mental health challenges, and I learned that prioritizing my relationship with him *helped* my mental health tremendously. This focus empowered us to be more synergistic in every other area of our life and relationship together.

My third vital priority was my children. I identified the priorities in caring for my children so that their needs–physical, emotional, and spiritual– were met. My children were dependent on me and their care took priority over any outside consideration.

Simply stated, those were my core priorities. I learned that there were times in the process when they were all I had the bandwidth to take care of— and that was acceptable to me on a temporary basis. Over time as I healed, I was able to expand my focus as my emotional and mental resources grew. But those top three priorities continuously took precedence over everything else, and still do.

Your priorities may be different from mine. As an individual, it's important not to compare what those non-negotiable items are. Make sure to ask yourself this vital question: *What self-care tools and what relationships simply **must** be prioritized and nurtured to optimize mental and emotional well-being?*

As you become clear about what matters most and you choose to put that first, it will help you eliminate many stressors and create a healthy, solid foundation that supports mental wellness. This is an empowering exercise I invite all my clients to do!

Mindful Evaluation

Even though the full map I've given you has specific steps, yours is a unique journey; as I mentioned, it will look different from anyone else's. Incorporating these vital principles will help your brain start to heal. Your sense of self will begin to come back to you. I promise, your natural sense of joy will reemerge too. You will physically and mentally feel more clear and empowered. What a beautiful thing!

As stressors come–as they do in any life–and you work through each learning point in the recovery cycle, understand that this is normal. I invite you to live mindfully and intentionally as you continue in your recovery from bipolar symptoms, celebrating new habits and applying new tools. Your key will be to create a habit of intentionally implementing evaluations on a regular basis.

When you are learning a new skill or modality, it becomes necessary to place *extra* focus on that effort. For example, when I was learning to use mindfulness meditation, I was spending time each week studying my book's designated chapter and then I set alarms to remind myself to do my morning and evening practices. Those were my priority during the eight weeks of the program. Upon completing the program, I reevaluated and adjusted my schedule to incorporate the tremendous benefits of mindfulness in a sustainable way.

You can regularly assess daily routines and commitments to make sure they are in line with your current priorities. I found the most effective tool for this process is a bullet journal. It is designed as a mindfulness practice that keeps me consciously aware of the choices I am making with my time and resources. I check-in with myself on a daily, weekly, monthly, and yearly basis. It also can be an "atta-girl" so I can see my growth.

I have tried using various calendars and planners over the years, but I found that those items tied me to someone else's structure that never fully supported me. When I first encountered the idea of bullet journaling, it was in a YouTube video where a woman was creating elaborately designed pages that looked beautiful but took forever to execute. This turned me off until I learned that it was just her *interpretation* of the method.

Bullet journaling is actually designed to be very simplistic. When I read Ryder Carroll's book, *The Bullet Journal Method*, I discovered the following: *"The power of the Bullet Journal is that it becomes whatever you need it to be, no matter what season of life you're in."* That sparked some genuine interest because that concept absolutely aligned with what I was so strongly discovering about who I was.

I stopped watching YouTube videos of the time-consuming, fancy page designs and focused on the basics. This is what Caroll suggested:

- An index at the beginning, to keep track of what I was writing on each page for easy reference.
- A "Future Log" so I would have a place to put items that I needed out of my head but weren't happening that month.
- A "Monthly Log" to do brain-dumps of what my mind thought needed to be accomplished that month.
- A "Weekly Log" for weekly items.
- A "Daily Log" to plan and keep track on a daily basis.

Sure, it took a hot minute, but learning to utilize a bullet journal simply yet consistently helped me regularly evaluate how my healing tools were working. If I needed to make adjustments in order to live a healthy, balanced, productive life, this was the best way to figure out what those looked like. Remember, too, that these check-ins are never a judgment of what you can or cannot accomplish: they are here to simply remind you of the balance you get to create to achieve the happiness you deserve.

Choose Your Hard

Recovery from bipolar symptoms was not an easy road. It took a lot of effort and determination, especially in the beginning because I didn't have anyone to show me the way. But every time I was discouraged or frustrated, I remembered my commitment I made to live for my daughter, for my family, and myself. I acknowledged that life with bipolar symptoms was already hard. Did I want the hard that meant perpetual suffering with no end in sight, or did I want the hard that could potentially lead to a better, more fulfilled life with the ability to create stable and joyful relationships?

My invitation to you is to consider this: your life is already hard. If you don't do anything, if you aren't ready to make any changes, it will continue to be hard. Do you want to stay living in the hard that never ends, or do you want to *choose* the hard that leads to healing and recovery? More and more of us are choosing the fulfilling hard, which becomes easier and easier in the long run, because you have put in the work and time investment in yourself. I promise, this is the hard that pays off.

Find Someone to Walk the Path with You

One advantage you have over me is that you don't have to figure this out for yourself! You will never have to walk the road to healing alone. I invite you to join The Upsiders' Tribe—an online community I designed to provide guidance, support, accountability, and encouragement as you walk the bipolar healing path.

The Upsiders' Tribe is a monthly or yearly membership program based on the steps in this book where you are given simple, actionable assignments. We meet virtually every week to share successes, ask questions, and receive encouragement from each other. You can find more information about the group on my website: www.theupsideofbipolar.com/the-upsiders-tribe

CHAPTER 12

YOUR JOURNEY BEGINS!

"Do you see her?" I asked Scott excitedly, leaning in and speaking loudly so that he could hear me over the noise of the crowd. I scanned the sea of red caps and gowns below me in the rows of chairs on the floor of the basketball arena.

"There she is!" I pointed when my gaze found the caramel-colored curls of my Gabby in the fifth row from the front.

"GABBY!" We all shouted together, arms waving wildly to get her attention.

My daughter turned and waved back, her smile radiant, her blue eyes shining. *My goodness, she's so beautiful!* I thought as I witnessed my little girl, all grown up.

The image of her dancing around giggling in the golden Belle dress with her halo of messy curls popped into my head. Tears welled up in my eyes and I said a silent prayer of gratitude that I was here today, healthy and whole, at my daughter's high school graduation.

I'm thankful that my daughter still has her mother, I thought, *and that I am alive and fully present today to celebrate* her *accomplishment. I'm just so grateful that I've healed!*

Sharing the Path to Healing

From the time of my diagnosis, I was repeatedly told three things: bipolar is a chemical imbalance, bipolar is like having diabetes and the medications are like insulin, and bipolar is chronic and incurable. As you know, I gradually discovered the steps on the path to healing and recognized I didn't have to continue to believe these lies. I realized it was possible to completely recover—far beyond merely learning to manage my symptoms.

Still, I didn't truly understand how far I had progressed in my healing until a family tragedy brought it to light. In March of 2020, we received the devastating news that my stepson Liam had ended his life. This heartbreaking experience was the worst trial of our lives.

In late fall of that year, I was on a run one day, contemplating the grief and emotional struggles we were all experiencing. That's when an epiphany struck me so hard, I had to stop on the side of the road to take it all in:

My depression in this situation is a normal reaction to this horrible event. This is not bipolar at all. This is life.

As I thought back over the previous months since we got the news, I realized with amazement that not only had I *not* completely fallen apart and become dysfunctional–as I would have in the past–but I was able to support my husband and children in their natural and normal grieving too.

Days later, in the full recognition of the incredible miracle of my recovery, I reached out to Dr. Davies to thank him. He was the one who had put me first when I brought him the information about Truehope. When I called his office, I was sad to learn that he had retired and his receptionist believed he may have passed away. As I hung up the phone, I sat in silence for a moment, filled with regret that I hadn't been able to express my gratitude to him.

I had hoped for Dr. Davies to understand how critical it had been for my recovery that he cared more about me than his ego as a medical professional. Putting my life first may have been a commonplace compassion for him, but he deserved to know that quite literally, he saved my life!

I wondered what would have become of me if this doctor hadn't been willing to consider micronutrient treatment. It was then, as I shuddered contemplating that horrible scenario, another thought came to life in my mind:

I need to teach other individuals with bipolar what I've learned!

A fire began to fill me. I started a blog titled My Upside of Down in December 2020. I imagined writing to my younger self, to provide the guidance and support I wish I'd had back then. All the while, I accepted the possibility that no one would want to read my blog, but if all that came from it was deepening my own understanding and ongoing healing, it would be worth making my struggle and perseverance public on the Internet, especially if it could help another person.

In the process of writing those blogs, I deepened my research of each of the tools I used in order to teach them more effectively. I was surprised to discover how many extensive, reliable studies had been conducted into each facet of my healing that proved their efficacy. **My experience wasn't a fluke; it was science!**

I found the path to healing bipolar, hidden in plain sight. It took me twelve years to find that cure, but after what we've started to embark on together in this book, you know it doesn't need to take that long for you. That's why I developed this map because bipolar does not have to be a life sentence! As I mentioned in the beginning, I went from feeling despair and hopelessness to living a joyful, purposeful life. Now you have the tools to choose that too.

Beginning the Path to Healing

Do *you* want to heal? I invite you first to ask yourself: why? Perhaps this may seem self-evident, but it's an important question to answer because the road to recovery from bipolar takes persistence and determination. Having a clear reason and intention to always keep trying, especially when it is most difficult, can help you persevere through challenges.

Recovery Cycle

Next, consider where you are in the *recovery cycle*. The fact that you are reading this book and have made it this far means you have likely moved beyond *precontemplation*—denial that you have bipolar symptoms.

Are you in *contemplation*—awareness that you have symptoms but still aren't fully committed to the healing? If this is the case, bravo for reading this book! What a great step on your journey. I celebrate that. I also want to acknowledge that sometimes people get stuck in this stage because of fear–fear of failure, fear you may never recover–and that emotion can be paralyzing. If this is the case for you, I invite you to take a simple action step today:

- Listen to my podcast The Upside of Bipolar where I have interviewed researchers whose books have supported my healing journey. This includes Dr. Bonnie Kaplan, Danny Penman, Robert Whitaker, and Dr. Ghada Osman, to name a few. This easy and powerful step can empower your move toward determination.

Are you in *determination*—you have decided you want to heal no matter what? Good for you! I celebrate that wholeheartedly too. Still, are you unsure exactly what to do next? Indecision and feeling like you need to keep learning (or somehow be perfect), before you start can keep you stuck in this stage. Make a choice to *do* something simple when you finish this book:

- If you are a mother or potential mother with bipolar, you can join my free Facebook group Bipolar Moms Learning to Live Well. This group is different from other online support groups I've encountered in one important way: we are not just commiserating in mutual suffering. We are providing hope and steps for healing!
- Download and use the free resource to create your Mood Cycle Survival Guide that can be found at www.theupsideofbipolar.com/free/

Keep it simple but whatever you do, *choose to act*.

Lastly, are you in *action*—ready to act on what you've learned? (Cue the heavenly chorus singing *hallelujah*!) Then you are ready for the Upsiders' Tribe!

- The Upsiders' Tribe is a self-paced, monthly subscription program that includes:
  - An online closed group forum and app for your phone.
  - Modules for each of the steps in this book with clearly defined, achievable weekly objectives to guide you through the healing process.
  - Once a month, thirty-minute, one-on-one success sessions to help you get the most out of the program.
  - Weekly group Zoom check-ins to provide participants an opportunity

to ask questions, be accountable for their progress, receive encouragement during learning points, and celebrate their successes.
- ° Periodic guest presenters to help you dive deeper into healing tools and resources.

I would love to see you there where we can continue this journey together.

Jennifer's Story

Shortly after I finished developing the beta version of The Upsiders' Tribe program, I was introduced to Jennifer. A beautiful, vivacious woman in her early twenties, she had been struggling with bipolar symptoms since her late teens. Like most of us, she found medications always made things worse. She had been unable to maintain steady work and was forced to withdraw from college and move back in with her parents.

When Jennifer asked if I could help her, I invited her to join The Upsiders' Tribe. She took her first step by developing her Mood Cycle Survival Guide (MCSG) with the help of her therapist and then began working with Truehope customer support to start cross-titration.

Jennifer shared her successes and struggles with me at our monthly success sessions. She consistently used her MCSG and then worked with Truehope to optimize her micronutrient intake. She also began learning how to use therapy productively to heal past trauma.

Over a three-month period, Jennifer noticed some dramatic changes. "It is amazing how much clearer my mind is!" she told me during one of our most recent check-ins. I loved the genuine surprise and joy in her voice as she shared, "I am able to resist the impulses that used to overwhelm me! I feel like I'm becoming the best version of myself!"

Jennifer has been able to maintain a steady job, a consistent daily schedule, and even equally exciting for her and her goals, she became engaged! "I'm inspired and so grateful that I can keep healing so that I can have a successful marriage and be a healthy mom to my future children." I celebrated that for her.

Public Speaking and Advocacy

As more people began to hear about my integrated treatment plan for healing, I was asked to share my experience and knowledge with local organizations. My first opportunity to do this was a women's group that did charity work in our community. I was thrilled with the chance to share my message and prepared thoroughly for the event.

I recounted my story and the steps to healing in front of a group of thirty men and women. Afterward, I felt so much gratitude for my ability to serve others as I finished with a powerful question and answer session with the completely engaged audience. I even spent an hour after the meeting speaking individually with almost half of the attendees.

One woman in particular approached me with tears in her eyes and said, "Thank you so much for your story and your vulnerability. I have been suffering from depression and anxiety for years, all on my own. When you spoke about your trauma healing, I realized that my symptoms are probably from my own unhealed trauma. I'm going to call my therapist on Monday and ask for help!"

Wowed at her inner revelation, I sincerely thanked her for sharing with me and asked if she would let me know how it went, handing her my number. Two months later, I received a text from her saying she had been working on processing her trauma and her life had already improved significantly. "I can't believe how much better I feel!" she reported exuberantly. "I am so much more patient with my girls and I feel more confident and happy. It feels like a miracle!"

Fight for What You Believe In

What are your hopes and dreams? Are they worth fighting for? What is it that matters most to you in your life? Is it worth doing the work to heal?

Now that you have been given the map–the steps to fully functioning, healing, and to claiming the beautiful life you were meant to live–the ball is in your court. You have the power to decide now how you want to move forward, knowing you will never be alone again.

Is "suffering well" good enough for you anymore? Or are you ready to take on your life like never before, choosing not to be relegated to myths and false beliefs perpetuated by an unhealthy industry, and instead choosing to **take control of your brain, your life, and your joy?**

I can tell you that healing feels miraculous. I never imagined in the early days after my diagnosis that I could live a healthy, balanced, productive life full of purpose and beauty, but here I am, and I can show you the way. It's time to heal and thrive.

Contact me!

- Check out my website for blog posts and resources: **www.theupsideofbipolar.com**
- Listen to my podcast: **The Upside of Bipolar: Conversations on the Road to Wellness**.
- Connect with me on social media:
    Instagram: **@upsideofbipolar**
    Facebook: **The Upside of Bipolar**
    YouTube: **@upsideofbipolar**
    X: **@UpsideofBipolar**
    LinkedIn: **www.linkedin.com/in/michelle-reittinger-upsideofbipolar**
- Contact me directly: **michelle@theupsideofbipolar.com**

I welcome you on this journey of healing and thriving. The more we do this together, the more we prove to ourselves and others what is possible. Join me!

APPENDIX
WORKS CITED AND ADDITIONAL RESOURCES

Chapter 6

Kaplan, Bonnie J., and Julia J. Rucklidge. *The Better Brain: Overcome Anxiety, Combat Depression, and Reduce ADHD and Stress with Nutrition* (Houghton Mifflin Harcourt, 2021).

Whitaker, Robert. *Anatomy of an Epidemic: Magic Bullets, Psychiatric Drugs, and the Astonishing Rise of Mental Illness in America* (Broadway Books, 2010).

Chapter 7

Greenberger, Dennis, and Christine A. Padesky. *Mind Over Mood: Change How You Feel by Changing the Way You Think, 2nd Ed.* (Guilford Press, 2016).

Van der Kolk, Bessel A. *The Body Keeps the Score: Brain, Mind, and Body in the Healing of Trauma* (Penguin Books, 2014).

Chapter 8

Williams, Mark, and Danny Penman. *Mindfulness: An Eight-Week Plan for Finding Peace in a Frantic World* (Rodale Inc., 2011).

Chapter 9

Nestor, James. *Breath: The New Science of a Lost Art* (Riverhead Books, 2020).

Osman, Ghada. *Mental and Emotional Healing Through Yoga: A Guiding Framework for Therapists and Their Clients* (Routledge, 2019).

Chapter 10

Heisz, Jennifer. *Move the Body, Heal the Mind: Overcome Anxiety, Depression and Dementia and Improve Focus, Creatively, and Sleep* (Harper Collins, 2022).

Chapter 11

Carroll, Ryder. *The Bullet Journal Method: Track the Past, Order the Present, Design the Future* (Portfolio/Penguin, 2018).

ADDITIONAL RESOURCES

Boardman, Megan. The EMDR Workbook for Trauma & PTSD: Skills to Manage Triggers, Move Beyond Traumatic Memories & Take Back Your Life (New Harbinger Publications, 2022).

Connelly, Jon. Life Changing Conversations with Rapid Resolution Therapy, 2nd Ed. (The Institute for Rapid Resolution Therapy, 2022).

Liebler, Nancy, and Sandra Moss. Healing Depression the Mind-Body Way. Creating Happiness through Meditation, Yoga and Ayurveda (John Wiley & Sons, Inc., 2009).

Whitaker, Robert. Mad in America: Bad Science, Bad Medicine and the Enduring Mistreatment of the Mentally Ill (Basic Books, 2019).

Moncrieff, Joanna. A Straight Talking Introduction to Psychiatric Drugs: The Truth About How They Work and How to Come Off Them, 2nd Ed. (PCCS Books Ltd., 2020).

---. The Myth of the Chemical Cure: A Critique of Psychiatric Drug Treatment, Revised Ed. (Palgrave Macmillan, 2008).

Schwartz, Richard. No Bad Parts, Healing Trauma & Restoring Wholeness with the Internal Family Systems Model (Sound True, 2021).

Tawwab, Nedra Glover. Set Boundaries, Find Peace: A Guide to Reclaiming Yourself (TarcherPerigee, 2021).

Williams, Mark, and Danny Penman. Deeper Mindfulness: The New Way to Rediscover Calm in a Chaotic World (Balance, 2023).

AUTHOR BIO

Diagnosed with bipolar disorder in 1998, Michelle Reittinger spent twelve agonizing years trapped in a relentless cycle of manic and depressive episodes, enduring a parade of therapists, doctors, psychotropic medications, hospitalizations, and suicide attempts. Overwhelmed by despair, she felt humiliated, hopeless, and lost, deeply pained by the impact her struggle had on her family—her husband and young children.

A turning point came when she and her psychiatrist discovered a groundbreaking approach that transformed her life. This marked the beginning of her development of an integrated method for understanding and treating bipolar disorder.

Now, as a passionate public speaker, author, and mentor, Michelle champions a revolutionary shift in bipolar treatment, focusing on healing and recovery. She emphasizes personal responsibility and challenges the victimhood mentality often associated with the disorder. Michelle advocates for an integrated, research-based treatment model that addresses the root causes of bipolar symptoms, paving the way for true healing.

Her greatest inspiration and motivation come from her family. Michelle credits her husband and four children as the driving force behind her perseverance and ultimate success in overcoming her struggles.

www.theupsideofbipolar.com
michelle@theupsideofbipolar.com

Reviews

"The Upside to Bipolar: 7 Steps to Heal Your Disorder is a powerful testament to one woman's extraordinary resilience and what can happen when we believe healing is possible. Michelle's story is a powerful reminder that the answers will come when we keep looking for options, no matter what hell we live through. Her seven steps give hope to anyone dealing with bipolar symptoms because they are recognizable, implementable, and repeatable for anyone willing to do the work necessary to heal! This book gets two thumbs up with my whole heart and mind!"

Wendy Beth Cozzens, Soul-guided coaching, #1 international best-selling author of *Living Blueprint: Five Principles to Creating an Authentic Joy-Filled Life*

"Reading this book is a great way to develop a new way of thinking about your brain health. Michelle Reittinger begins with her personal story: how she discovered that her pharmaceutically oriented doctors were wrong about bipolar disorder being a permanent state–recovery is possible. Then she provides you with her Mood Cycle Survival Guide: steps to follow to move toward that recovery.

This book will give you a new perspective of what is important for your brain health: from foundational micronutrients to mindfulness and yoga, and from exercise to adopting a healing mindset. It's all here, showing us that we can all do many things to heal our brains. Buy this book and reclaim your mental health!"

Bonnie J. Kaplan, PhD, coauthor of *The Better Brain*

"The Upside of Bipolar transcends being merely a collection of therapeutic tools or a personal testimony; it is an extraordinary blend of both. Michelle Reittinger invites us into the deep intimacy of her life journey. Rather than battling the symptoms of bipolarity, Michelle embraces them, using them as guides to navigate the intricate landscape of her mind, body, and spirit, leading to profound healing over traumas.

Michelle Reittinger takes us to the threshold of possibility, where bipolarity is redefined—not as a life sentence or stigma, but as a space brimming with hope and learning. Here, she charts a path for readers to follow, offering them a map toward their own healing journey."

Sophie Rouméas, Happy author, transgenerational & mindfulness coach, hypnosis practitioner

"Michelle is such an inspiration! Her genuine heart and voice shine through as she shares the challenges and lessons that she has learned through her fascinating life. This book and Michelle's journey can be helpful to people who struggle with a variety of mental health issues, not just bipolar disorder! I also feel that it can be helpful to family members who are wanting to support a loved one with mental health struggles, so they can better understand their loved ones' experience. The practical suggestions on how to improve mental health are explained well and many are easy to begin to use and implement. The book really shows that with effort, persistence, and support, it really is possible to live well after a mental health diagnosis. The hope this offers is invaluable."

Julie Sickles, LCSW

"For individuals living with bipolar disorder, Michelle's book is a beacon of hope and a practical guide. Her insights into the holistic management of the condition can be instrumental in finding and sustaining stability. Mental health professionals will also find The Upside of Bipolar to be an enriching resource. Michelle's firsthand account enhances the understanding of the patient experience and underscores the power of a holistic, individualized treatment plan."

Dr. Jennifer Giordano, psychiatrist

"I was sucked in from the very first page. Even though I have been thriving in my own life while living with bipolar for the last twenty years, Michelle shared some new ideas and helped me see ways I can go even deeper with my own management and knowledge. Her honesty, determination, and even skepticism when approaching new ideas made me trust her more as a legitimate source of helpful information."

Mequell Buck – Author, public speaker, suicide survivor, and founder of Mental Illness Warrior

"Michelle was told she would never get better. She came to reject that narrative of illness and drug treatments, and instead fashioned a holistic path back to wellness: exercise, micronutrients, and mindfulness were three of the 'steps' that worked for her. That is the gift of her story: it replaces a narrative of illness told by psychiatry today with a narrative of recovery and healing."

Robert Whitaker, Author of *Anatomy of an Epidemic* and *Mad in America*

"The birth of resilience!

Michell took me on an incredibly intense, turbulent journey. This demon that chased her around for much of her adult life was very real and present and had a massive hold on Michelle's life and everyone connected to her. In a desperate attempt to find peace, doctors continually led her down a path of prescriptions and invasive procedures to fix her bipolar disorder; instead, it kept her flirting with taking her life numerous times. Michelle authenticates to the reader how important it was for her to relentlessly search for a holistic alternative solution and found it. She put together a very comprehensive, well laid out plan to help and support anyone suffering.

Everyone needs to experience her struggle and triumph! Her husband, Scott, restores all faith in humanity. He teaches unconditional love, empathy, and undying support throughout the entire journey. The pain we go through is a resurrection of our faith and these two are an example of that.

Michelle, thank you for being vulnerable and giving each of us this gift of understanding, healing, resilience, persistence, and will to live!"

Jason M. Palmer, Master horse trainer, consultant, trainer and coach, #1 international best-selling author

"This book is a game changer for its holistic and healing approach. This is a must buy, read and share with anyone you care about living with bipolar disorder."

Maureen Ryan Blake, Maureen Ryan Blake Media, and #1 international best-selling author

www.ingramcontent.com/pod-product-compliance
Lightning Source LLC
Chambersburg PA
CBHW020355130626
46549CB00006B/2292